River Dreams

River Dreams

The Case of the Missing General and Other Adventures in Psychic Research

Dale E. Graff
Former Director of Project STARGATE

ELEMENT

Boston, Massachusetts • Shaftesbury, Dorset
Melbourne, Victoria

© Element Books, Inc. 2000
Text © Dale E. Graff 2000

First published in the USA in 2000 by
Element Books, Inc.
160 North Washington Street,
Boston, Massachusetts 02114

Published in Great Britain in 2000 by
Element Books Limited
Shaftesbury, Dorset SP7 8BP

Published in Australia in 2000 by
Element Books Limited for
Penguin Books Australia Limited
487 Maroondah Highway, Ringwood, Victoria 3134

Library of Congress Cataloging-in-Publication data available

British Library Cataloguing in Publication data available

Printed and bound in the United States by Edwards Brothers

ISBN 1-86204-716-2

Previous book by Dale Graff

Tracks in the Psychic Wilderness

Dedication

To my wife and family, for their understanding and encouragement of my explorations.

To my canoe partners, Carl Schmieder, Fred Nelson, and Brian Gnauck, for their companionship on the great wilderness rivers of Canada.

To Rhea White for encouraging me to share my experiences and explorations.

To all explorers seeking to extend the boundaries of our inner domain.

Something there is that doesn't love a wall,
that wants it down.

—Robert Frost
"Mending Wall"

Contents

Preface

River Dreams explores our psychic nature from a personal perspective. The true-life incidents in this book are those I experienced or directly observed. I include some activities from STARGATE, the U.S. Department of Defense's former program for research into applications of remote viewing. I describe a variety of incidents from personal, professional and research experiences that illustrate the range of psi* phenomena. Some of these, such as intuition, synchronicity, extrasensory perception (ESP), remote viewing, telepathy and precognition provide information. Others such as mind–matter interactions (psychokinesis) appear to be energetic effects. I prefer the neutral term *psi phenomena* for all the experiences described.

I believe that a close link with our natural world helps us uncover psi talents in a comfortable and balanced manner. I consider implications from concepts in quantum physics and new innovative areas of study to help in our understanding of psi. And I include philosophical musings throughout the book that reveal the depth of my own search for understanding.

We can experience our psi nature in two ways: while awake or during dreams. While awake we can have a sudden hunch, impulse or feeling, or encounter a synchronistic event. We can be in various

---

* Psi, the 23rd letter of the Greek alphabet, was designated by British parapsychological researchers in the 1940s as a neutral label for psychic phenomena. Parapsychology is the science that studies psi. See Glossary for terminology definitions.

degrees of relaxation, even deep meditation states, when psi events occur. While asleep, we can experience psi in ordinary dreams or in lucid, or conscious, dreams (when we know we are in a dream). In this book, I focus on both dreamtime and incidents of conscious-state psi, but for most people, the easiest and most reliable way to experience psi consistently is during dreams.

In my previous book, *Tracks in the Psychic Wilderness*, I explored our natural psi talents from a neutral perspective and provided approaches for uncovering remote viewing, psi dreaming and synchronicity. It is my objective in *River Dreams* to show that anyone can be his or her own psi sensitive—including you. The most useful psi application is in precognition—future seeing. By exploring your future-seeing nature, you keep a step ahead of the surprises coming your way. Some of them may be undesirable and can be avoided. Some offer opportunities that may go unnoticed without an alert from your inner self.

As we discover the reality of that "helping hand" that psi can make available, we come to see the value of psi for both the great and the small incidents. We are entering an increasingly complex global society with many competing (and potentially threatening) aspects that can at any time affect our personal well-being or even our safety. By opening up and working with our psi talents, we can improve the efficiency of routine activities. Our decision making can be enhanced, since we are drawing on all the potential data available to us. We can quickly respond to unexpected crisis situations to avoid serious injury. In some instances our foreknowledge can have life-saving potential for ourselves or for loved ones, or even for strangers. As more of us accept psi's help, we come to experience a deeper sense of connectivity between all life forms that hints of a co-creative aspect of the universe. We discover that we can have a role in evolving our own and society's future in positive cooperative directions. *River Dreams* will help you understand that we can access psi's helping hand and thus be better prepared to ride the fast currents coming our way.

Appendix A has an approach for uncovering future-seeing psi talent. Appendix B has recommendations for achieving goals and well-being. Appendix C offers an opportunity for you to "Try Your Psi."

Psi does not exist only to be an interesting anomaly. There are no useless phenomena in the universe. Psi provides a subconscious interface for linking us with others and our environment. I have come to accept our psi potential as a natural part of the universe. The phenomena are neutral and democratic. Enhancing our creative, intuitive and psi talents provides help to meet the challenges of the twenty-first century.

Anyone can dream *river dreams* and receive the knowledge they carry along. *River dreams* help us to understand ourselves, others and the universe we live in.

Introduction

I often dream of rivers. They meander through my dream landscape, moving through hidden places, forming pathways that take me into a deeper wilderness within. I travel on them to see what I can discover, to learn what can be learned. After these river dreams, I return to the place where I began, to ponder the experience, to wonder anew, and to seek ways of bringing some essence of the river's secrets into waking life, into ordinary reality.

I also travel on the rivers of this reality. Although I prefer primitive settings, especially those in the north woods and in the Arctic tundra, I seek most any river. If I cannot travel on them, I walk along their boundaries, gazing at their sparkling water, listening to their murmurs as they glide over smooth pebbles or to their thunderlike beckoning where they plunge over a high falls into a deep pool.

At rivers, I hear music that resonates with an ancient beat; I discover a sense of poetry as rhythmic words flow easily through my mind. I feel the river's powers, too. Its energy enhances my own, and I feel empowered. I look downstream toward some distant horizon to where it, or I, am going, and wonder about the forces that relentlessly move me along the river path that I have chosen to travel. I look upstream, curious about the river's origin, and the origin of all life, all things. From what deep spring did the river, or I, emerge?

Rivers can reflect our moods. We feel what they seem to feel: confidence when they flow steadily, uncertainty when mist-covered, peace when drifting through places of beauty. Then we sense creation's mysteries and our connections to all things.

Some rivers reveal what we wish not to see. They may be stagnant, stuck between narrow constricting canyon walls. Or they may have absorbed debris and pollution that they carry into other rivers at some distant confluence. They can spread out and choke life in nearby streams.

Many rivers are pleasant to travel on and lead us to new possibilities. They pulse with living things; they run fresh and clear, drawing nourishment from hidden springs. Their channels are flexible; somehow they avoid or repel the silt from other rivers.

Sometimes I travel on gentle streams, gliding silently with a slow current, studying the river's path and the landscape it reveals. Other times I travel on racing rivers, totally focused on the river itself, on its swirling and pulsing waves, on its obstacles. On such rivers the channel may be narrow and twisting and require all the energy and attention I am capable of achieving in order to navigate safely. I do not fight such rivers. Instead, I seek a way to cooperate with them, to face directly what I can. I merge with the river path and avoid what I cannot navigate. Sometimes such rivers have places that must be bypassed. There are warnings—a telling roar, a rising mist in the distance. Then I come to shore, walk around the danger, and continue on.

Occasionally we misjudge the river's current. We may move into it too quickly when not adequately prepared. As the current speeds we may need to backpaddle or angle into a calm bay and search for a better channel. We discover new boundaries—those of the river and those within ourselves. Sometimes we are caught or trapped in the powerful flow of a large river and can only plunge ahead as best as we can. When that happens, we can still be alert and look for unexpected help or discover a way through the turbulence.

Rivers can toss surprises in our path. Maybe a sharp turn reveals unsuspected vistas or lets us glimpse something unfamiliar. Sometimes the river twists too sharply and we are face to face with swirling water that forms countercurrents and whirlpools. Vortexes spin from such dynamics and can be very powerful. To pass around or through them we need to keep balance, find the best channel, and focus totally on the goal of successful navigation. For a moment we merge with the surging river, we become partners with it, we allow it to help us move safely downstream. There is much to learn from such rivers.

As for me, I have discovered that rivers of this reality have much in common with rivers from within—those hidden channels of our mind. As we travel external rivers we learn balance and cooperation. We discover the importance of focus of intent and goal setting. Then when we seek to travel on inner streams we are better prepared. We can respond to the flow, to the surprises, to the challenges, and get safely through whatever turbulence we may encounter. We return enriched with new understanding, even new talents. We learn about our interconnections with others and our environment. We experience the flow of life and discover the far reach of our subconscious mind through unknown rivers that pulse deep within our psyche.

I have come to know two types of rivers—those of this world and those springing from unknown regions within our psyche. These rivers are part of our natural world, our natural universe. We can travel on both of them, and learn from them. Dreams are like rivers. They are windows that let us see the currents within our mind.

River Dreams can lead us into new regions of our unconscious and into our deeper nature. They can be experienced by anyone.

PART 1

Deep Currents
and
Hidden Rivers

A ll rivers have currents. In broad, level channels, they move slowly along the surface and are difficult to notice. In steep, narrow channels, they run deep and penetrate into hidden depths. Psychic rivers also have deep currents that penetrate into an inner domain where sources of information and energy can be found.

Sometimes river channels penetrate through hidden passageways into other rivers, and their currents merge. Similarly, we can cross boundaries in our psyche and merge with information in the environment or with information known to others. The more powerful and energetic the situation or the more critical the need, the more likely it is to be sensed.

In this section, I discuss several incidents that illustrate the role of emotions and need in facilitating psi perceptions for experimental projects and for "real" distant areas or activities. I present examples from my own explorations in *Mental Resonance* and from the STARGATE program in *Fire!*, *Airplane Down*, *Search for General D.*, and *On The Run*. They have details on the searches for a missing Soviet airplane, an abducted Army officer (Brigadier General Dozier), and a fugitive wanted by the U.S. Customs Service and the Drug Enforcement Agency (DEA).

chapter one

Mental Resonance

φ

In 1976, I made a canoe trip on the Coppermine River, which flows into the Arctic Ocean through Canada's Northwest Territories. Before the journey began, I made arrangements with Harold Sherman, renowned author and psi sensitive from Arkansas.[1] He had agreed to seek psi impressions of me and our small canoe group three times a week, while he remained at his home in Mountain View, 2,000 miles south. These impressions were sent to Dr. Harold Puthoff at the Stanford Research Institute (SRI) in Menlo Park, CA, where they were notarized and filed. After completion of our journey, I retrieved Harold's impressions to see how well they correlated with actual events.[2] He had experienced several highly specific impressions that could not have been guessed. He succeeded in tracking us during our river journey.

I was at the beginning of my STARGATE career, having recently been appointed as the government's contract manager for remote viewing research at SRI. Harold Sherman's tracking experiment gave me insight into remote viewing's potential for search and rescue missions—potential that we later realized in our research and applications work for the Department of Defense.

The term "remote viewing" was adopted in the early 1970s by physicists Dr. Harold Puthoff and Russell Targ and their research team at SRI. We continued to use the term in STARGATE, to represent the informational aspect of psi.

When I returned from the Coppermine River journey, I made an extensive review of hundreds of experiments at SRI and developed plans for new research. These experiments demonstrated the reality of remote viewing and that it had the potential for search and rescue missions. But precise data, especially of an analytical nature, was difficult to produce consistently and sort out from incorrect impressions.

Remote viewers' sketches were more reliable than their verbal interpretations, or naming, of the sketches. Basic shapes that they drew usually correlated with the forms and patterns present at the target area, but they could be misidentified. The psi process—like any type of activity—is influenced by a variety of physical, psychological and neurophysiological parameters.[3]

Individual differences in cognitive styles and background affect the nature of psi data. As in anything being learned, psi can be improved or uncovered with practice. Some individuals did not need any focused approach for uncovering their psi talents. They had the appropriate neurophysiological networks already in place, usually from childhood or from years of activity that required reliance on their intuitive talents. One of the talented early SRI remote viewers, Pat Price, had been a very successful policeman who routinely relied on his hunches. Other talented individuals were successful in artistic careers (Ingo Swann, Hella Hammid) or excelled in some analytic profession such as mathematics (Gary Langford) or psychology (Keith Harary).

Their styles were quite different. Some preferred to describe or sketch geometric features of the distant places; others preferred a wider range of "sensing," such as feelings, sensations, movement, sound, smell or taste. Some preferred or performed better with only the observables of the distant place; others preferred the idea of establishing contact with people who were present—the beacon person or sender, the outbound experimenter, or others.

Some psi sensitives believe that the psi process is enhanced through rapport and trust. Others believe that psi is essentially independent of establishing rapport. From what I observed, connectivity to a distant environment through something like a consciousness hologram and linking with information known to a distant person are two possible sources for psi data. It may be that "thought" has wave-like properties similar to how a hologram functions. Aspects of our "thoughts" could interact with a region or field (a consciousness or subconscious field) that, similar to the physical spacetime nature of reality, extends or can manifest throughout the universe. Such a field would contain the accumulated knowledge of all minds in a type of "psi space." Another concept of the psi process is that we are accessing own future knowledge through precognition. Picturing "consciousness" as a "field" can be a meaningful conceptual model for the psi process. In this view, "mind" is perceived as not restricted to the physical limitations defined by the brain.

As I continued to work with psi-talented people, I wondered how widespread psi ability was in the general population. Maybe more people had repeated psi experiences than I suspected but were unwilling to talk about them. I wondered if people who were not aware of experiencing any psi could do so when they were open to the possibility and given the opportunity.

To gain insight on how widespread psi talent might be, I scheduled a *Psychic Realm* program through an educational facility in the Dayton-Beavercreek, Ohio area. My purpose was to present information on psi, including the critics' objections, and to provide opportunities for attendees to take part in psi experiments. I included the history and current status of psi research, reviews of spontaneous incidents that were reported in the literature, and a variety of background material from philosophical and metaphysical perspectives. I did not emphasize any single interpretation or concept; I suspected (and still do) that no one can really explain psi or attribute psi to any belief system.

I designed my psi experiments to be as comfortable and neutral as possible and made no assumption as to what style or approach was best for anyone. Participants were free to describe the unknown (to them) place or picture—the target—either in the waking state or in the dream state. They could be totally awake, slightly relaxed, or in a deep meditative state. They could seek ordinary dreams or lucid dreams of the target. I explained basic approaches for the awake and the dream option.

For remote viewing, I asked them to simply relax, set a desire to "access or describe the target," shift focus inward, and take note of any emergent impression—visual, feeling, thought or other sensation—no matter how vague. For seeking dreams, I asked them to set a firm intent to recall any dream relevant to the intended target and to record it as soon as possible upon awakening.

Since I had complete control of the targets, it did not matter when during the week they attempted the experiment. I urged them to try the experiment as soon as they could, following class, while enthusiasm would still be high. I requested that their impressions be mailed to me for record-keeping purposes and to facilitate review the following week.

The targets were either real places in the local area, photos of a scene or slides with a variety of features. Earlier I had made a list of a variety of diverse sites in the local area and then randomly selected one of them as the target for each experiment. After selection, I visited that place and remained there for at least fifteen minutes, focusing on class members and wishing them success. My role in observing and interacting with the site or picture as a beacon person was believed to help facilitate the psi process. For pictures and slides, I simply observed them while remaining in the comfort of my home. I would look at some of them as a beacon person and keep others sealed so that I could not know their contents. A colleague prepared a large selection of pictorial and slide targets. Some of the slides were from the same target pool used by the Maimonides Medical Center in Brooklyn, NY, for their dream telepathy and awake state research.[4] I had no knowledge of the target content.

I facilitated the *Psychic Realm* course for five years until I moved from Dayton to Washington, DC. Sometimes I held two programs at different times of the week at different locations. Each program ran one evening a week for ten weeks. Attendance ranged from 20 to 30 participants. On the average, I discovered that at least a third of the attendees did well on my psi experiments without extensive practice. Sometimes, participants would not show any evidence of psi until late in the program.

As a result of these *Psychic Realm* classes, I came to the conclusion that psi talent is widespread in the general populace. Those who did well on most of my projects had a history of spontaneous psi experiences, especially in the dream state. Working with pictorial targets was easier and more interesting to the participants than were local area targets. Pictorial targets were easier to evaluate, since they usually had unique features that could not be easily guessed. My *Psychic Realm* programs were appreciated, and I gained much from helping people uncover their own psi talent or overcome cultural negativity. Working with local people gave me confidence in the experimental data from the SRI researchers. Obviously, psi ability is not reserved for the self-proclaimed superstars but is potentially available to any one of us. All we have to do is be open to the possibility and practice, always evaluating suspected psi information to be sure guessing or inferences are not responsible for the results.

During *Psychic Realm* programs I observed that the students' success with my targets did correlate with the type of target and with my own degree of involvement with it. Targets that had little appeal were not usually sensed. Those that were interesting, that had a variety of contrasts and real or implied activity, were usually sensed accurately. Sometimes the exact nature of the target was not perceived, but the emotion or dynamics were experienced in imagery with which the individual was familiar or comfortable. If I put a lot of energy as a beacon person into visualizing the target and its activities, more class members were accurate than when I gave little attention to the target. However, some participants did well even when I only glanced at the target picture or when the pictures were sealed and I did not know what they were.

My procedure for picture targets was to hold focus on the picture for at least fifteen minutes starting at 10:00 P.M. following each class. In addition to the picture's content, I recorded any impressions or associations I had that were not apparent from elements in the picture. These included related memories from similar places. In some cases, I envisioned specific actions that were consistent with the scene.

For local remote viewing areas, my procedure was similar to that used with pictorial targets. In some cases I scheduled my visit to the target place during daylight on the day following the evening class. I had learned that it was not a good idea to loiter in front of some buildings in the evening. Sometimes a patrol car would stop to investigate and occasionally some unruly individual would approach.

One of the early psi experiments for the *Psychic Realm* program was a picture of a volcano erupting at night. This was the first target with vivid contrasts and implied intense dynamics. It showed lava shooting skyward in a thin fiery column. Irregular rivers of lava flowed down the volcano. As I observed the picture, I envisioned the lava surging like a cascading river, pushing and tumbling large lava rocks from left to right. I envisioned the volcano erupting and filling the sky with streaks of fire.

Eagerly, I awaited their letters with impressions about the target, wondering if anyone had sensed any aspect of the volcano. As the letters arrived, I could see that class members would be in for a surprise. Some of the waking state impressions during the time I was observing the picture were:

> *Suddenly I see Fourth of July fireworks exploding in the sky.*
> *I am skiing down a mountain. Something very sluggish flows*
> past.
> *Something like a colorful water fountain . . . pulsing up and*
> down.
> *I hear a rushing noise . . . then thunder-like booming sounds.*
> *Something dark flies up in the air.*

A few class members who had been open to dreaming the target wrote:

> *I am traveling somewhere and it is very dark. I am standing at*
> *the edge of a large river. The water rushes past and I feel the bank*
> *begin to crumble.*
> *I am standing in a railroad station. Suddenly a train rushes*
> *through. It is being pulled by an old-style steam engine that belches*
> *huge columns of smoke and steam. I feel the ground tremble.*

Some of the other letters had elements of the volcano target but also contained a variety of other descriptions that had no clear association to the volcano. As I reviewed these letters, I saw that my volcano photograph was a good target and gave class members evidence of their own psi abilities.

At the next class, I wrote out a summary impression on the blackboard from the letters I received and then asked class members to select the actual target from among three other possibilities drawn from my target pool. They had little difficulty selecting the correct picture. This experiment provided convincing evidence to the class members that almost anyone could experience psi under appropriate conditions. I knew that one demonstration could not serve as proof. There were various potential technical difficulties; my target pool was small and not completely uniform; or there might have been a television program on volcanoes the night of my experiment. In the weeks that followed, the class members improved with practice, and a few of them were consistent and accurate.

Success with the volcano target picture suggested that the dynamics implied by the picture, or by what I envisioned, were important to the psi process. This led me to conclude that our psi nature functions very much like our other senses; vision relies on edge and motion detection, hearing on changes in air pressure. Our senses are wired to detect changes. The erupting volcano had distinct visual boundaries; my envisioned motion imagery may have added to the detectability of those boundaries. The black and red contrasts were stark features that may have helped class members to sense the target's basic nature.

Regardless of what is detected by our psi sense, the basic psi information is usually presented to our consciousness, whether awake or in a dream, in terms of our individual memories and associations. These impressions can be very accurate, approximate or symbolic. The approximate or symbolic impressions may only represent aspects of the target, perhaps as a result of weak psi connection or perhaps to shield the true nature of the psi information from consciousness. The psi target may invoke a disturbing memory or possibly something that may be perceived as a threat. If the psi target has high emotional content, it may be interpreted in a form with which the individual is comfortable.

For the volcano target, no one perceived it as a volcano, even though their impressions were representative of the volcano's activity. It was clear to me and the class that some of the participants had sensed the essence, the gestalt, of the target picture. Some impressions were more distorted, or disguised, than others. A psi-talented geologist steeped in volcano dynamics might have sensed the target exactly.

Over the years, I observed similar patterns in the psi responses from other *Psychic Realm* psi experiences. Targets with vivid, implied motion or that evoked strong emotion like *Volcano* were usually easier for class members to perceive than those that were bland. Targets with distinct geometric features and vivid colors also led to good responses, even though they lacked apparent motion or emotion content.

The most consistent result was the inaccuracy in how participants interpreted the nature of the target picture or place. The sketches would have good correlations, but participants usually could not name the target object, scene or place. The SRI remote viewing research led to the same conclusion.

There were instances where the target pictures or places were perceived correctly. I suspected in those cases that the individual had prior associations to them. A target picture of the Grand Canyon would be easier for someone who had once visited that area. Sometimes the targets would be self-evident, such as the Statue of Liberty. Even faint or approximate impressions could lead the perceiver to name the target correctly.

After several *Psychic Realm* classes, I began to notice that some people did better when I was observing the target than when I had selected one randomly and not opened the envelope. These class members preferred to rely on rapport for establishing a type of mental resonance—something like telepathy. They may have been accessing my knowledge of the target, or maybe I served as a type of "beacon" to help them locate the target. They usually sensed a target's emotional aspects more easily than its geometric or shape properties.

In one experiment, I selected a relatively neutral scene—a picture of Red Square. The picture showed the entrance to the Kremlin on the left and Lenin's tomb on the right. It was taken when only a few people were in the square.

The class responses were interesting. Some of the participants perceived a *plaza area* or a *large-walled building*. One of the respondents had a dream:

> I am walking through a small building that is like a hospital. A very pale man is lying on a bed. Someone has died here. I walk through this building several times.

She went on to describe foreboding feelings and woke up feeling disturbed. Her dream did not portray a plaza or any other aspect of Red Square. I had not focused on Lenin's tomb. I certainly knew it was there and may have had negative subconscious associations that she sensed instead of the neutral configurations of the plaza and Kremlin I had intended.

I encountered several instances in which I thought the target picture was neutral but instead some nonobvious emotional aspect was sensed by the class participants. In those instances, either I had a potentially negative memory association or the participant did. I could not anticipate those incidents and could only hope my targets would not stir up anything too disturbing. I became extremely conscious of the emotional aspects of my experiments and in no way wanted to have class members seek psi impressions of something potential disturbing, such as a bloody scene. By now I had established rapport with class members, and as they opened their psi receptivity, any psi experiment could lead to surprises. These unexpected intrusions were usually easy to reconcile and were often quite humorous. In a few instances, they were not.

Occasionally, my randomly chosen target would be a peaceful lagoon, usually a *National Geographic* picture from an article about a

Pacific island. Though lacking in strong emotion, these scenes were good targets since they had high visual contrast and clear boundaries—mountain, curving shorelines. Sometimes surf action was visible. Class members generally did well on this type of target picture.

In one instance, the response from a participant to a peaceful lagoon was startling. As I held focus on the peaceful lagoon, I found my thoughts drifting from the target picture to memories of when my wife and I nearly drowned in a Hawaiian riptide. It occurred to me that if I held my breath, I might be able to generate more intensity than usual. Perhaps depriving oxygen flow to the brain—as occurs during drowning—would look like a mental call for help to their psi sensitivities. So I held my breath for about a minute as I gazed at the peaceful lagoon picture. Then the phone rang.

"Stop it, stop it! Stop whatever you are doing! I feel as if I am suffocating! I can hardly breathe!" screamed the voice on the telephone.

I was stunned. It was Kay from the *Psychic Realm* class. She had earlier shown preference for the emotional aspects of psi targets and certainly picked up on emotion in this instance.

"Kay, please calm down. Detach from this experiment! Nothing is happening . . . and please do not continue it!" I said loudly and firmly.

In a few moments, she regained her composure. We talked for a while, and she assured me she would not try the experiment again. I learned later that no one else responded with the same intensity as Kay, even though some of them did describe bay-like scenes.

The next evening I called Kay. It had taken only a few minutes to overcome that intense reaction to my experiment. Even though she had not desired any further impressions, she did have a brief dream about a relative she had not thought of in years—a child who had drowned. We had a long talk about this experiment. It seemed that she had picked up the intensity of my "riptide" recollections and the effects—whatever they were—from my breath holding.

This dramatic experience brought a realization of how our thoughts can be sensed by others even when they are miles away. Even though I had detected specific intentions, including negative thoughts from others while dreaming, I had not seen evidence that these thoughts could cause disruptive effects. Kay's reaction to my traumatic memories showed that under certain circumstances psi impressions can be perceived as disturbing.

Since no one else taking part in that psi experiment reacted negatively, I concluded that Kay's tendency toward dramatic reactions in ordinary situations and her highly developed psi sensitivities had led to her intense response to my target. Her filter for emotional material was probably not as effective as it should have been. She wanted to be as accurate as possible, and her strong intent to know the target may have amplified its traumatic themes. Her interest in rapport and its implications for mental resonance may have added fuel to the fire. As I reviewed this incident, I could not be sure how much of Kay's reaction came from my own traumatic feelings and my breath holding, and how much came from her sensing the basic incident and recreating the trauma of a drowning from her own memory and imagination.

I began to explore ways for gaining insight into the source of psi data. Prior to my *Psychic Realm* courses and SRI remote viewing research involvement, all of my personal psi experiences had a known individual as a potential psi source. But some of my *Psychic Realm* targets and many of the SRI projects showed that it was not necessary for someone to be observing the target. Individuals with psi talent could still describe the target, although their sense of what it was— their naming it—was almost always incorrect. This suggested that the role of an observer or beacon person might be for additional knowledge. That is, psi sensitives might be accessing the meaning of the target from the observer's knowledge. The target picture or place and the observer's knowledge can be avenues for psi sensing. The preferred route to the target may be person-dependent.

I wondered what would happen if someone devoted a lot of intention to accessing a target unknown to anyone. What effect might that have on the type of target information perceived? So far, class participants' responses to double-blind targets—those unknown to me—were emotionally neutral, although they tracked the geometrics of the target picture. But that may have been due to expectation. I had assured them the targets my colleague prepared would be safe and nonthreatening. I did not want to turn my class into an experimental laboratory. Nor did I want to set up formal experiments to explore this question with the SRI remote viewing researchers. Our formal research was restricted to the remote viewing approach, which downplayed the target's emotional content.

I set up a few psi projects that I could explore alone. I had my colleague prepare the target material from pages torn at random from magazines in the dark so that he could not be aware of anything in the target pool. I planned to explore these double-blind targets in both the relaxed and the awake state at convenient times. To initiate the task, I randomly selected one of the sealed unmarked envelopes from the box of targets he had assembled and placed it out of reach on a high shelf in my study. I selected the target in the dark for extra assurance that there was no normal way I could detect the sealed envelope's contents. Later experiments were also successful when I had colleagues in distant cities prepare and select the targets to see if distance had any effect on results.

In one of these experiments, as I was focusing on the target, the only images that I perceived were *small objects on thin long stems, like signs.* The objects were *round and seemed flat.* Later, I focused on having a dream relevant to the contents in the sealed envelope. Late that night, I had a vivid dream:

> *I am in a canoe on a swift-moving river, trying to paddle out of the current. There is something wrong with the paddle blade. It is loosely attached to the handle, and I cannot exert any force. I take a*

closer look. The blade is round and has a large hole in it that allows water to flow through. I grab another paddle that is very shiny and reflects the blue color of the water. I look up and see a strange-looking airplane glide by. Its wings seem to be rotating.

If my impressions were of psi origin, then the hidden target emphasized many odd, flat shapes. The dream action called attention to paddle shapes and paddle-like motion. I knew the shapes were not paddles; their configurations and their shiny, colorful surfaces indicated they were for some other purpose. The dream lacked emotion; the action seemed too gentle for real water dynamics. I did not sense the presence of anyone and thus suspected the target picture was primarily of unusual objects, probably an art form or abstract painting. I thought it might have something that resembled an airplane, but the wings of my dream airplane were not like real wings. My paddling action did not imply that people were in the scene. I had noted from past experiments that I usually play-acted something about the objects in the picture to dramatize their general configuration.

After I sketched the images from my relaxing period and the dream, I wrote a summary in my journal and retrieved the sealed envelope. The moment of truth had arrived. I tore open the envelope and gazed at the target picture. It was a full-page advertisement for weather vanes!

They were of unusual designs—round or slightly elliptical and mounted on thin rods that formed a ninety-degree angle with the vane. The one on the top of the picture was shaped like an airplane. Its wings were round cylinders designed to roll in the wind. The larger of the elliptical-shaped vanes had a large hole in the middle. They were mounted in a row against a blue sky background.

Now I understood my presleep imagery and the shapes I saw in the dream. My dream conveyed the basic essence of the objects—something that moved in a stream—but I missed the nature of their purpose and the medium in which they were intended to move. My sketches were close approximations of the larger vanes. I was pleased with this result. Now I knew that I could also access a target that no one was observing. I had experienced a type of mental resonance with something inert.

Even though I had seen striking examples of remote viewing of distant scenes from the SRI research, I considered someone's knowledge somewhere—even a bystander—to be a possible source of remote viewing information. With double-blind target pictures, there was not even an innocent, unwitting bystander.

I had to pursue this independent double-blind experimentation to be sure I had not made a lucky guess. But I was not guessing. I was basing my conclusions on imagery I had experienced in a relaxed or dream state.

Some weeks later I set up another double-blind target. I was very busy with work and social activities and could not get into a relaxed state. So I held strong focus before sleep for perceiving the target picture in a dream.

I woke in a few hours from a dream that was difficult to recall:

> *I am in a dimly lit classroom, not paying attention to the lecture; it*
> *is on a political science theme topic that I do not find interesting.*

This dream, if it related to the target, was too vague. I often had classroom dreams and would not see this as evidence for psi contact with the target even if some aspect correlated. I again held focus on trying to perceive the target in a dream. But I could not return to sleep. Occasionally, I held focus on seeing the target picture but experienced no imagery.

After a long time, I put on my glasses and looked at the clock. It was 3:00 A.M. I did not want to be awake all night. Removing my glasses, I again held focus on the target, hoping to drift to sleep. It was

Friday night, and I wanted to close out the experiment and not repeat it the following evening. I remained in bed, intently hoping to perceive the concealed target picture. Gazing at the opposite wall, I wondered when I would fall asleep.

> *Then the wall disappears! I am aware of the bed, furniture and the other walls. But the wall directly ahead is not there. In its place is a thick black void. Then something like a long dark tunnel forms. In the distance, I see a small light area that expands and becomes a scene. A long row of wide, stone steps appears and comes into the bedroom. At the far end, near a large dome-shaped building, I see a small figure. It begins walking slowly down the steps toward me. As it approaches, I clearly see that the figure is a stocky man dressed in an old-style military uniform. His chest is covered with decorations, and I note a large buckle on his belt. He is wearing a flat-topped hat. As he approaches, I can clearly see his face. His demeanor is not friendly, but I feel no fear. Then he stops at the foot of my bed. I watch, amazed, as he raises a submachine gun to his shoulder and blasts it directly at me! Gunfire sound fills the room. I see the fire spit from the gun and feel the impact from at least six bullets as they tear through me.*

Suddenly, the attack scene vanishes and I am looking at the bedroom wall. I could not believe what I had just experienced. The entire episode seemed real, including the impact I felt when hit by the bullets. For an instant, I thought I had actually been shot and was now dead. But I was able to move. Quickly, I jumped from bed, put on my glasses, dashed into the bathroom and turned on the lights, expecting to see a bloody mess. The only effects from the shooting that I could detect were about half a dozen reddish welts on my chest. They looked like burn marks.

I turned on the room lights, and recorded the entire experience in my journal. This incident seemed to be a conscious or lucid dream that evolved from a relaxed state before I fell asleep. Even without my glasses on, the entire episode was in clear focus. This was a highly dramatic and emotional experience. I could only hope it related to the unknown target and not to some emerging physical situation.

I returned to bed but could not sleep. Half an hour later, I rechecked my chest, and did not see any traces of the odd red welts. I fell asleep and woke around 6:00 A.M. from a long dream:

> *I am in a large, old building, looking down at a dark street. I see a crowd of people in dark clothing who appear threatening. A dark-haired woman is with me, who seems concerned about something. We talk of political issues and make plans for a political rally. Suddenly, the people in the street attack the house; I hear shouting and window glass breaking. The woman screams and panic surges through me.*

I quickly recorded this disturbing dream. It had a political theme consistent with the first dream and possibly with that vivid shooting experience.

Early that morning I retrieved the sealed envelope and went to Lofino's coffee shop in the nearby Beavercreek shopping center. I had lots to ponder. If my dreams and the waking dramatic imagery were relevant to the target picture, what might it be about? The vivid conscious dreamlike experience with the military figure had to be a major clue. I suspected the military man was a well-known war per-sonality. The long stone steps and dome-shaped building suggested something ancient, but that contrasted with the machine gun. If the gun was on track, then the target picture might depict something from World War II. I did not recognize the stocky man but suspected the shooting action had to be a significant target picture element—that is, assuming the experience was target-related. I remained highly concerned as to why I had experienced a shooting scene—including being shot—so vividly! Maybe a physical problem was emerging and I should schedule a physical checkup.

I was not sure how to interpret the dreams. They both conveyed political or military activity. The first dream was detached and academic. The last dream had activist flavor, but it did not seem to be of a military nature—contrasting to the dramatic shooting in my conscious dream. These dream experiences hinted of a World War II setting, but I was sure the military figure was not Hitler.

After pondering the possibilities over several cups of coffee, I had to open the envelope and learn the truth. Finally, that moment of high anxiety had arrived. I retrieved the sealed envelope from my briefcase and tore it open.

The target page had a black-and-white picture of Mussolini walking down wide steps in Rome! He was dressed in a well-decorated military uniform and was wearing a flat box-style hat. A long sword dangled at his side. Waves of relief flooded through me. That dramatic experience was not about me! So why had the experience ended in that terrifying shooting episode that seemed powerfully real? Maybe I had misinterpreted his sword as a gun. Even so, why would I overdramatize the weapon aspect of the target picture?

I purchased another cup of coffee as I continued to review these experiences. Suddenly I remembered—I recalled an association to Mussolini that was like a buried memory.

When I was twelve years old, a few of my friends and I peddled our bicycles to a nearby county fair. Several unusual sideshows attracted our attention. One of them announced *The Last Days of Mussolini.* Thinking this would be a fun thing to see, and expecting a rip-off with only a few WW II photos pinned to the canvas tent, we were in for a shock. In the center of the tent was a casket. In the casket was a wax model of Mussolini depicting his appearance right after he was assassinated. I stared at his bare bullet-ridden chest! The wax figure was extremely realistic. It had huge purple circles surrounding the depressions around his heart where the bullets had hit. I left that sideshow extremely agitated, imaging how horrible it must have been to be shot like that.

Now, some thirty years later, I reexperienced the trauma I had felt when I saw that display of Mussolini. That memory of Mussolini must have surfaced to convey the exact identity of the figure in that target picture. The temporary red welts may have resulted from mental energy I gave to this experiment and my intense desire to know the target. I have observed hypnotists give someone the suggestion that a cigarette was lit when it was not—resulting in small burn welts appearing where it touched their skin. My temporary wound marks were the same phenomenon.

The traumatic lucid experience with the target picture gave me insight into similar unusual experiences. I had been curious about stigmata phenomena—the appearance of deep wounds on certain historic mystics when meditating on the crucifixion event. I had thought of such accounts as unreliable. My *Mussolini Encounter* demonstrated to me the power of our subconscious for creating vivid theaters of the mind and for dramatically influencing our physiological processes in observable ways. *Mussolini Encounter* was a lucid or conscious dream experience: I remained aware of the bedroom. The entire episode may have been a conscious dream, including my perception of the bedroom.

Mussolini Encounter reinforced my conviction of the power of the mind. We can use this power for self-healing, or we can use it for self-slaying if we dwell on negativity.

The ordinary dreams that same night also made sense. The target page was part of an article on Mussolini and the circumstances leading to the fall of his Fascist political regime in Italy. One of the paragraphs presented a vivid account of the attack on the building in which his daughter, a major party personality, had been staging political action. My last dream conveyed the essence of that incident.

I now could put closure on my nighttime adventure with that unknown target picture. My ordinary dreams were on track. My conscious dream, *Mussolini Encounter*, was certainly an intense mental resonance experience. And the only mind involved was mine!

Mussolini Encounter provided additional insight into unusual experiences sometimes perceived by some people as "UFO abductions." Are these "abductions," vivid as they are, really intense and dramatic conscious dreams? What happens if someone with strong interest in UFOs were in the presence of others who were equally if not more intensely interested in this subject? What if emotional material, such as is presented by sensationalistic books and television, were nearby or recently seen? Would it not be likely, with those conditions of emotional energy and expectation, that the subconscious mind creates a dramatic UFO abduction experience in the theater of the mind as a conscious dream?

φ φ φ

I continued working with that double-blind target pool. Most of my targets were geometry-rich, such as scenes, structures or geometric designs. My waking impressions or dreams were relatively neutral and usually correlated well with the target picture elements. A few generated emotional responses, but the resulting dreams were not lucid or conscious dreams.

On the night of one of these experiments, I woke from a strange dream right before the alarm rang:

> *I am walking through a wide, open field with several thin, tall white columns. I notice a sign and walk toward it. I cannot see it clearly but have the feeling that it is a warning about the danger zone I am in. I sense a type of health hazard and begin to feel sick.*

I woke up feeling very nauseous. After a few moments, this odd sick feeling subsided, and I felt fine.

The target picture was a full-page cigarette advertisement. It showed a pack of cigarettes with a smooth green cover. Several cigarettes protruded from the pack. An easy-to-read sentence covered the bottom of the page: "Warning: The Surgeon General has concluded that cigarette smoke is hazardous to health."

The thin, tall white columns in a green field resembled the pack design and the extended cigarettes shown on the advertisement. I now understood the source of my temporary nausea. As a nonsmoker, I had taken the warning notice literally and experienced the printed message as a sick feeling. I did not recognize any of the signs or words in the dream, and I did not know the thin white columns were cigarettes. At some level I had discerned the Surgeon General's warning note. My nausea was similar to what I had felt when I first tried smoking as a teenager. I had become sick and did not continue smoking. (To this day, I cannot tolerate cigarette smoke.)

In this experience with the target, I could only identify shapes and colors much as impressions are perceived in remote viewing experiments. My subconscious mind sensed the meaning of the printed warning and presented it to me consciously as a feeling. That feeling came from my memory of how cigarette smoke had affected me some thirty years ago. I added the feeling association; it did not come from the cigarette target page. The visual information—the picture and words—came from that page. I did not think I had accessed the target through precognition of my future knowledge when I later opened the target envelope. Otherwise, my future knowledge would have recognized the thin, tall white columns as cigarettes.

If I subconsciously understood the Surgeon General's warning, why did I not recognize the cigarettes in the dream? It took the entire dreamtime period for me to grasp the meaning of the words. A different mental process may be involved for word recognition that I did not integrate with the picture-making process. Feeling associations were easier and quicker to convey to my consciousness.

I suspect that had I focused on having a "second opinion" clarifying dream, the Surgeon General's message would have been presented in easy-to-understand cigarette smoke imagery. I am glad I did not seek a follow-on dream. I have no tolerance for secondhand smoke, even in dreams.

φ φ φ

During this time, I made contact with Diane, a psi-talented individual from my Air Force organization. Our exploratory psi experiments were with locations in the Dayton, Ohio area. She was very accurate in her impressions and reinforced my conviction that psi had potential for Air Force missions such as locating missing airplanes or pilots. Since we were sure such opportunities would arise, we continued practicing with a variety of psi targets.

One of our work colleagues, Ray, an Air Force lieutenant, was planning a short visit to Michigan. Why not have him select a target place, while he was traveling, for Diane to describe via remote viewing? Ray looked forward to his "beacon person" role, and Diane felt challenged by the distance.

Ray agreed to select a target place that could be anywhere in Michigan at the agreed-upon time of 6:00 P.M. on Saturday. I asked him to prepare a list of ten diverse target possibilities, select one at random, and then drive to that place.

Diane agreed to sequester herself in a quiet place at her house shortly before 6:00 P.M. and seek psi impressions of the target place that Ray was looking at. As a backup, she also agreed to seek target impressions of the remote place in a dream, should something unforeseen develop with her schedule.

That Friday evening, Diane, Ray and I met to establish feelings of confidence and connectivity. Ray wished Diane well, and I could tell he was very excited at being part of this experiment. Though skeptical of psi, Ray had a positive attitude and was able to suspend judgment. He planned to return the following Tuesday, and we agreed to meet at noon over lunch to discuss results of our first long-distance remote viewing experiment. I would have no contact with Diane until Tuesday noon.

That Saturday, I played tennis in the morning and worked in the yard during the afternoon. Later, I wondered if Diane had perceived anything during her long-distance remote viewing session. I looked forward to learning ground truth Tuesday noon. I had no intention of trying to seek impressions of Ray's target; however, my curiosity may have won out. Late Saturday night, I became aware that I was experiencing a conscious dream:

I am in a large airplane that is open at the back. I walk toward the opening and fall out. As I am falling toward the ground, I clearly see a mountain below that is sparsely covered with small trees. I look above and see a large multicolored shape that looks like a parachute. Someone is nearby, also falling, but I do not recognize the person. I continue falling. The mountain zooms toward me. I know I am dreaming and decide to leave the dream.

Then I am aware of the bedroom. It is 4:00 A.M.

That conscious dream was extremely vivid and realistic. I could only wonder what it signified. It felt as if I was skydiving. In my nightstand notepad, I sketched the scene. Even though I had no intention of recalling more dreams, I woke right before the alarm from another dream:

I am a passenger in a car that is parked along a dark city street. Something on the dashboard catches my attention, and I lean forward to see what it is. Suddenly, a door opens and something like a sheet of paper is blown out of the car and falls to the curb. I lean over and look under the car but see nothing.

This dream was hard to recall. I had no personal associations to it and did not understand the symbolism or action. I recorded both dreams in my journal but could think of no reason for them. I had not seen any recent television programs or read anything that resembled parachutes or skydiving.

I knew that remote viewing of distant locations can occur in a dream state and that it can be retroactive—that is, for places someone had visited in the past. The content of my conscious dream ruled out anything Ray could have been doing. So what was that odd conscious dream about? I did not think it represented something symbolic about me; I knew that dreams of falling were not uncommon.

Tuesday noon finally arrived. Diane was early and apparently quite anxious. She did not seem very confident and resisted talking about the results of her remote viewing attempt. Ray arrived on time, but he did not seem as optimistic as he had prior to his trip. Neither one wanted to initiate the discussion.

"Well," I finally said, breaking the ice. "Let's see what happened on Saturday. Diane, let's hear from you. Were you able to do the remote viewing experiment?"

She was slow to respond. I wondered what had gone wrong.

"No . . . Sorry . . . Our visitors from out of town stayed longer than we expected. I could not break away at 6:00 P.M. to do the experiment," she said, hesitantly.

I was disappointed but kept a positive outlook.

"That's OK, Diane. We'll go at it again. I'll set up another long-distance experiment."

She smiled, and nodded slowly.

"By the way," I asked cautiously, "did you experience any dreams that might relate to Ray's target place?"

"Well, nothing relevant." She paused, not sure whether to proceed or not. "But I did have a crazy dream. I know it had nothing to do with Ray's target. I don't know what to make of it . . . it was really strange."

Something was beginning to make sense.

"Diane, why don't you describe it? Some aspects of your dream might correlate. Let's see ..."

"There is something else," she quickly interrupted. "This was not an ordinary dream. I have not had one like this since childhood. It was like a lucid dream, or conscious dream as you call them. It was really weird."

Ray and I sat quietly, wondering what strange tale she was about to relate. "Diane, if it is too personal, we do not want to know," I said cautiously.

"Oh, no! It is not personal. But ... well, OK. Here is the dream," she said, as she opened a file folder and pulled out a sheet of paper. "You are in for a treat," she said, grinning. "Let me read it."

Suddenly I am aware that I am high in the sky! Nothing is holding me up and I begin falling toward the ground. I look down and see a huge mountain. I can see gullies and slopes. I look up and see something like a parachute, but I am not attached to it. The parachute has many colors. Someone else is nearby, but I cannot see who it is. Then I am falling faster and see the mountain approaching. I stop the dream.

She put the paper down and glanced at us. I was elated. We had experienced similar conscious dreams! I quickly explained my conscious dream. Now Diane was intrigued. How could this happen, when I had not even been intending such an experience? I showed Diane and Ray my sketches; she gave us her sketches. They were nearly identical.

"What time did you have your conscious dream, Diane?" I asked, curious.

"Oh, I definitely know the time. It was exactly 3:00 A.M.," she said, emphatically.

I was surprised at the one-hour difference between her dream and mine. They were identical in structure and action but not in time.

We had almost forgotten about Ray. I glanced at him; he seemed a bit pale. "OK, Ray, let us hear from you. I am sure you would not do anything as shocking as skydiving during a remote viewing experiment. A beacon person is not supposed to do stunts or take risks," I said jokingly.

Ray seemed subdued for a few moments, shaking his head slowly from side to side. "I thought I had blown the experiment!" he exclaimed.

Diane and I stared at him, puzzled, waiting for him to continue.

"You see," he mumbled slowly, "on Saturday I became sick—some type of fast-moving virus or something. I did not have the energy to set up remote viewing targets and almost called to cancel. I was fortunate to schedule a doctor's appointment for late Saturday afternoon and was barely able to drive a few miles to the office. As I was in his waiting room, an idea came to me. Why not choose a picture as my target place? That would be easy to do. I could visit it in my mind even when sick."

Diane and I listened silently, ready for anything.

"But I had no set of pictures with me for targets. So I picked up one of the magazines in the doctor's office and paged through it until I found a real doozy of a picture!"

From his enthusiastic remark, I could tell what he was about to say.

"You see, I tore a page from the magazine and gazed at the scene on it, intending it to be Diane's remote viewing place. After a few minutes I folded the page and put it in my coat pocket. It was around 5:00 P.M., but I did not think that mattered."

"Yes. Yes, Ray!" shouted Diane, impatiently. "What was the picture? Let me see it!"

"The picture I chose showed a hot air balloon race," he said firmly. "Several balloons are high in the sky above a large mountain somewhere in the Southwest. If you only glance at the picture, it gives the impression of parachuting or skydiving. Your sketches of what you called parachutes resemble the balloons! The mountain you two sketched also resembles the one in the picture. I only glanced at it, an hour before our remote viewing appointment."

Diane and I sat quietly, absorbing everything he described.

"It looks like you two did not even need me to look at that page," he said wryly. "And now I can't even show it to you."

"What do you mean?" quizzed Diane, as she gazed intently at him.

"Well, as I said, I was not feeling well. I left the doctor's office a bit disoriented. But I did remember the target picture and placed it on the dashboard of my car to remind me of our 6:00 P.M. appointment. I planned to look at it when I got to the pharmacy."

"So . . . sounds like a good idea," acknowledged Diane.

"Well, it wasn't," said Ray cautiously. "You see, when I opened the car door, a strong wind gust caught that page and snapped it out of the car! I thought it went under the car. I crawled around trying to find it. It was nowhere in sight. "

"You mean . . . you lost the target picture?" exclaimed Diane, disappointed.

"Yes, I did! Sorry. But I remember the magazine, and I am sure we can get a copy from the local library."

Then I recalled my last dream where something on the dashboard catches my attention, like a sheet of paper that is blown out of the car. Now I understood; my dream had tracked Ray around 6:00 P.M. and conveyed information about the type of target he chose and how he lost it.

I showed Ray my journal and let him read that dream description. After finishing, he sat quietly for several minutes as if unsure what to say.

"I really cannot believe this! Did you two have someone follow me?"

We knew he was jesting, but his reaction was typical of many who experience accurate psi data for the first time. "Yes, Ray, we did follow you, as we had previously agreed. We followed you in psi space or wherever psi information is stored. So you were 200 miles away; what did that matter?" I said in a matter-of-fact tone.

Ray was uncomfortable with his "close encounter" with psi. He probably had not thought the experiment would succeed. We talked a long time about the implications of psi and the benefits that our psi potential can offer to ourselves and others. All we have to do is be open to the possibility and go do it.

As Diane and I left my office, Ray quipped, "OK . . . OK, all I can say is this: Please, you two, get on the search team should I ever become lost in the North woods."

"Or even in Detroit!" I retorted.

We all laughed loudly, pleased at the results of our surprising psi experiment.

We met again the following noon. I had found the magazine with Ray's target picture in the Beavercreek library. We wanted to take a closer look at our sketches and the picture. Both Diane and Ray were able to reconcile the experimental results. Diane had felt uneasy about the conscious dream mode. This experience gave her better understanding of many of her disturbing childhood incidents that she had misinterpreted as being "out there," and not from within her own mind-theater. Ray, being a recent physics graduate and electro-optics specialist, had difficulty reconciling psi. He did acknowledge that there is much we do not know about the universe and that science does not have all the answers. Our experiment, and the research material I had been giving him, showed him that there is more to our nature than we generally assume. He could now accept the reality of psi and had responded in a sensible way—critical but not supercritical. Put psi to the test. Be an experimentalist. Take a look before passing judgment.

We studied the picture and could see that our sketches did match the target elements very well. That visual feedback gave us new confidence and enthusiasm for continuing our psi exploration.

As we were about to leave, Diane burst out laughing. Others in the office area glanced around, wondering what was happening. Ray and I were puzzled. Diane continued to stare at the target picture.

"OK, Diane, what is so funny? Falling from the sky does not necessarily create humorous feelings," I protested.

"Look. Look at the caption to the picture at the bottom of the page!" she exclaimed.

Ray and I stared at it in disbelief. The balloon race was photographed in Colorado . . . at *Sleeping Giant Mountain!*

Now we understood. Could it be that our subconscious psi process had a sense of humor? Did we have those unexpected conscious dreams to let us know, via a humorous synchronicity, that the most important aspect of the target was not a balloon or the sense of skydiving. It was a specific mountain. We had been falling into a *Sleeping Giant.*

We sat quietly for some time wondering about the implications of our interesting psi experience. We had learned something about the nature of our deep subconscious mind. We all have a *Sleeping Giant* within us, and our inner giants are there for us to welcome, unafraid. As we parted, I thanked Ray for choosing an outstanding target and being a great beacon person.

"Yeah, right, anytime," he laughed softly. "Anytime. Glad to be of help."

φ φ φ

That evening, I walked to a stream in the nearby forest, pondering our experiment. Several layers of mental resonance had occurred—with Ray, Diane and the environment. Our mental resonance can be for the great and the small, for something important or for routine information. All we need to do is become explorers and discover for ourselves the range of our connectivity. Then we can experience the nature of those rivers flowing deep, and eternally, within our psyche.

I glanced at the small stream, musing:

We can all dream of rivers,
Rivers can dream of us,
And carry to anyone the dreams of others,
And the dreams of Giants.

I returned refreshed and eager to continue with *river dreams*.

Fire!

φ

E vents that entail strong emotion are easier to perceive than incidents involving low emotion. Our ordinary attention is more easily drawn to emotional or dynamic situations than to trivial incidents, allowing easier recall. But highly emotional situations do more than enhance memory. There is something in our psyche that facilitates an easier recognition, or reception, of a distant emotional situation. The emotion we experience may be from the remote incident or it may be from our memories of something similar that help us interpret the psi perceptions.

Some types of emotional situations do seem to invoke consistent responses in psi sensitives, especially if the intensity is high. Fires, earthquakes, floods or any type of personal threat can act like a bright beacon in psi space. A type of highly energetic physical signal may occur that interacts with the medium or "field" by which psi information is transmitted or perceived. Emotional response reactions may result from the detection of rapid physical changes in the environment.

Fire can be easier to detect through psi than other types of emotion-generating incidents because the concept of fire is an innate aspect of our subconscious. Most of us have had the experience of "being drawn" toward fire—around a campfire, relaxing by candlelight, or simply lying in the sun on the beach. But our relationship with fire has deeper roots. Fire has been a central part of all mythological and religious traditions for millennia. The image of fire is a permanent part of our personal and collective psyche and often invokes a mysterious, all-powerful feeling. We are warmed by fire, yet we are fearful of it—it fascinates while it threatens. Our survival "fight-or-flight" syndrome plays a role in how we respond to fire, but there is more to it than that. Fire resonates with something within us that we fear or fear we cannot control.

Fire is also a dream symbol for personal change—the trial by fire, the inner transformation. This has obvious physical counterparts, such as fire for melting or transforming compounds to extract pure elements. Any inner change process can invoke fear—we really do not want to change; we are not ready to be "re-formed" in any way. Fire is physically and emotionally easy to recognize. It should be no surprise that fire is easy to perceive through psi no matter how distant in time or place.

A good example of how someone can sense a distant fire via psi perception is Emanuel Swedenborg's experience. In 1759, while he was 300 miles from his home in Stockholm, Sweden, he experienced a visual image of a fire raging in Stockholm. He kept track of its progress, noting that it came to within three houses of his. Later that day, messengers brought the news of the fire, as he had described.

John Dunne, British engineer, had many dreams of distant fires and disasters before news articles appeared, including the eruption of Mt. Pelée in 1902.

One does not have to be a seer like Swedenborg to sense a distant fire. Many cases exist in psi literature illustrating how people with no suspected psi sensitivity sensed remote fires threatening a friend, a loved one or even a stranger.

Dr. Louisa Rhine, pioneer parapsychology researcher, examined 10,000 cases of realistic and symbolic spontaneous psi events. Over 50 percent of the most dramatic experiences were premonitions of fire.[5]

Detecting fire is common in spontaneous psi accounts, but what about fire as a target in an experimental situation? At first, I thought fire had to be an actual occurring event in order to evoke a psi response, but while working with a varied set of pictures used as psi targets (i.e., the pictorial target pool), I noticed that even a picture of a fire was easy to detect in psi experiments, even for novices. It did not seem to matter whether the picture was being observed by someone (i.e., a sender or "beacon" person) or retained in an unopened envelope with no one knowing the contents. Somehow even the unobserved picture of a fire came through loud and clear!

The *Volcano* experiment during my *Psychic Realm* course had alerted me to the strength of a fire picture. A few weeks after that experiment, I had a fire dream:

I enter my Psychic Realm classroom and glance around. Someone is missing, but I am not sure who it is. I walk to the blackboard to write summaries of the psi target impressions that were sent to me during the week. Switching on a slide projector, I click four slides onto the blackboard. They shift to the right side, and the last one extends from the blackboard into the right-hand corner of the room.

The first slide is a city scene from a low altitude. I see a wide river in the distance and a stadium in the foreground. The second slide shows the same scene but has a thin column of black smoke rising high into the sky. The third slide shows an oddly shaped black car emitting smoke from its trunk. The fourth slide shows the car

*parked on a curving road, completely engulfed in flames! As I
observe this slide, it becomes dynamic, like a movie, and I feel
intense heat from the car fire. I back away from the blackboard and
the projected scene. I see thick black smoke rise from the car and
swirl into the sky.*

I awoke feeling as if I had just came from witnessing a fire. I could
still feel the heat that I experienced during the dream and could still
hear the crackling noise of the car being consumed by fire. This was a
surprising dream; I recorded it in detail in the morning for later
analysis. I did not feel disturbed by the dream, even though the dream
dynamics seemed threatening.

The dream scene of a wide river and stadium reminded me of the
Ohio River and Riverfront Stadium in Cincinnati, Ohio. I had no
plans to visit Cincinnati and had no association to the type of car I had
seen in the dream. The dream hinted of a psi origin—the *Psychic Realm*
class setting, my intention to write psi inputs on the blackboard, the
visual slide format of information projection (like remote viewing). If
it was psi information, who or what was it about?

The dream began with the sense that someone was missing from
my psi class. This hinted that the dream was about one of the class
members. If so, was it about something that had happened that Friday
or earlier, or about something in the future? Did it have warning
potential? As I thought about the different class members, I recalled
that one of them had talked of having relatives in Cincinnati. I planned
to ask her at the next class if my dream had significance for her.

I did not need to wait until the next class; she called me the next
day. She wanted to tell me of a disturbing incident that had occurred
to her and her husband that Friday evening. I listened, intrigued, as she
explained what had happened. They had gone to Cincinnati that day.
On their return, as they were entering I-75 in Cincinnati, a large black

car stalled in front of them, blocking traffic. The driver let the car drift backwards to the right side of the ramp. As traffic was about to pass on the left, fire erupted in the rear of the car. The gas tank exploded, and the car was engulfed in flames. Fire raged, and tires began burning, emitting columns of thick black smoke. People stuck behind the burning car had to back down the ramp to escape the heat. In moments, fire trucks arrived and sprayed chemicals on the burning car. When the smoke cleared, only a charred mass remained. No one was injured, but the emotional level of those witnessing the incident was extremely high.

Now I understood that strange dream of Friday night. Even though the *Car Explosion* dream occurred at least ten hours after the incident, it still conveyed the intense feelings and emotions she and her husband had felt earlier. The slides in the dream conveyed accurate information on the location and on the specific incident.

Her participation in the *Psychic Realm* course, her interest in psi and the intense emotions invoked by the car fire created favorable conditions for my spontaneous psi experience. The distance could have been much farther, even thousands of miles, and the dream would have been the same. Fire, even the threat of fire, is a bright beacon in our emotional landscape—for this reality and for psi space. I recently had a fire dream of a potentially serious situation. This dream, *Car Fire*, depicted a fire hazard with my car's fuel pump, which was later confirmed. I had it replaced before it caused a fire.

The threat of fire can lead to life-saving action. A colleague of research chemist Rita Dwyer had a disturbing fire dream in which he saw Rita enveloped in flames from a chemical explosion. The next day, an explosion occurred in her laboratory and fire spread rapidly. Her colleague had been on the alert for something unusual because of that warning dream. When the fire erupted, he was able to respond quickly and rescued her from the flames.

Fire can emerge in our dreams in powerful ways even when there is no personal significance or any distant or emerging fire threat. One puzzling and unusual fire experience dream occurred during an experiment when the target was a slide in a sealed envelope drawn from a target pool prepared by a colleague. The envelope was randomly selected and secured in a distant part of the house. My dream objective was to "dream about the hidden target slide." I only recalled one dream right before waking:

> *I am standing at the shore of a wide river looking at wavelike*
> *ripples that reflect orange-red colors. A few large boulders are in the*
> *foreground, extending into the river. As I observe the scene, the*
> *intensity of the light increases. I look up and see that the cloud-filled*
> *sky is becoming very bright. Low on the horizon, I see a glowing*
> *object that increases in size until it explodes! Instantly, I feel*
> *scorched by intense heat as the entire sky erupts in flames. The river*
> *reflects a deep blood-red color, and the earth trembles.*
>
> *The scene disappears, and I am looking at the headlines of a*
> *newspaper. Bold print announces that a "war has erupted." I strain*
> *to read the details and sense that the conflict is in the Mideast.*

When I awoke, I still felt the sensation of scorching heat experienced during the dream. Even though I could vividly recall the dream imagery, I could not remember all the words I had seen in the newspaper. The dream invoked an intense feeling of doom that stayed with me most of the day.

The dream, *Nuclear Explosion*, emphasized destruction and fire. I did not think the dream related to the concealed psi target slide. The dream was highly dramatic and filled with intense feeling and emotion, not typical of my psi dreams of concealed slides. Target slides thus far had not contained printed material. I was sure the dream was not about me, since I was only an observer. I wondered if the dream was precognitive of a future global incident. Was World War III about to be initiated somewhere with the use of nuclear bombs? I did not feel very good about this dream no matter how much I tried to symbolize it away. First, I had to rule out at least one possible dream source: the hidden slide target. I hoped that there might be at least some association with the target.

I retrieved the sealed envelope and opened it. To my surprise, the target slide was a picture of a beautiful sunset. The sun appeared as an intense glowing orange-red sphere low on the horizon. Brilliant colors reflected off a cloud layer and from the ripples on a river in the foreground. Many boulders extended into the fast-flowing water.

I had sensed all the key aspects of the hidden target slide, but my dreaming mind turned its peaceful scene into a holocaust. My day-to-day work with weapon systems assessment may have predisposed me to associate nuclear explosions with the sunset on the slide. Dreams are storytellers. My subconscious mind needed a context—the best analysis or interpretation to fit the basic impressions. Weaponry was easier for me to anticipate than a real, peaceful scene. But what is the sun? Maybe an aspect of my subconscious that generated dreams (my dream maker) had correctly identified the essence of that glowing sun—nuclear fusion! Thus, my error was one of scale, not basic interpretation.

Was the last part of the dream a projection of Cold War mentality due to the explosive implications of the slide, or did I resonate with something deep within me or our collective unconscious—the fires and explosions of primal creation? Is the threat of a nuclear war and the fear of a holocaust much more intense in our psyches and closer to our consciousness than we realize?

As I reviewed possible interpretations of this intense dream, *Nuclear Explosion*, I gradually accepted its intensity as primarily of my own doing. The slide was a catalyst that rang my psyche's (and psychic) chimes. I was not absolutely sure. Maybe there was a war approaching, somewhere. . . .

Three days later, I had my answer: Mideast conflict had erupted. The writer of the news article described it as an emerging World War III. Fortunately, this conflict, the Six Day War, ended quickly.

I do not think I could have guessed that the Six Day War situation was imminent. This new conflict flashed bright and intense and was over within a week.

I took another look at *Nuclear Explosion.* Now I understood what had happened. In opening up my psi scanning process for accessing that concealed target slide, I linked with themes—explosions, war— that were similar. The approaching real war had undercurrents of a possible nuclear holocaust. The themes fit, but the specifics were only partially correct. On the night of the *Nuclear Explosion* dream, my subconscious psi process resonated with several aspects of fire that were close together in psi space—that region of a consciousness hologram accessible through psi.

Fire reaches into the far depths of our psyche; it resonates with our conscious and subconscious fears and with those from possible future situations.

φ φ φ

In my psi experiments, I developed a preference for concealed magazine pages as psi targets. Even though methodological problems exist with this informal approach, I found it challenging. It offers the potential for insight into the psi process not available through structured laboratory experiments or even from spontaneous psi experiences. The material on the hidden pages can be extremely varied, including pictures or printed material or both. The scale of the pictures can vary from a full page to only a portion of the page. Occasionally, the pages are essentially blank or the picture is not very interesting. There was no way to anticipate what might happen during these experiments:

> *I am standing at the edge of a wide field observing golden grain that extends to the horizon. A golden-haired youth walks toward me through the field from the far left side. He is happy and conveys a sense of well-being. There is a circular tunnel entrance in the center foreground. I approach this dark opening and enter. I travel slowly through this dark tunnel. Suddenly, fire appears ahead and I see paper burning. The edge of a page peels back, and I can see through the tunnel to a natural scene. There are several people near a forest sitting on the ground. They seem to be digging at something.*

I woke from this dream with an intense feeling of joy and freedom. The dream scenes were beautiful and serene. I felt a slight tingling upon waking—often a sign that the dream was of psi origin. The fast pace of the dream was similar to that of many of my psi dreams. I was certain the dream had captured the main aspects of the concealed target page. What about the tunnel and the fire? Those elements were out of context. Maybe there was a dark cave-like area somewhere on the picture. The fire was odd; I did not feel any heat as I watched the flame burn away a page. I did not suspect a real fire was portrayed on the target page, and I did not sense a bright burning sun anywhere.

When I opened the sealed target envelope, I discovered the target was a full-page advertisement for Kodak film. The top half of the page showed a large wheat field ripe with golden grain. A young boy was standing in the field at the upper left side, breaking wheat heads. In the center of the page was the front view of a camera with a dark circular area depicting the lens. Words describing the scene and extolling the virtues of the camera and film appeared on the lower part of the page.

As I studied the dark lens area, I knew what my dream maker had done: That lens became a tunnel for moving to the other side of the page! The target page had, symbolically, been burnt and peeled back. I flipped the page over to the opposite side. It was a photo of naturalists examining plants near the edge of a tropical forest.

Now I understood all the elements of that dream. I had accessed the hidden target, and also perceived the content on the opposite side of the page. To help me know when this shift had occurred, my dream maker supplied transition clues—the tunnel and fire. For this dream experience, tunnel and fire had a much simpler role than their usual metaphysical interpretations. That is the nature of transition symbols; they are universal and readily available as clues for any change—for the great and the small. They are not to be taken literally, but they do point toward some type of basic change process or shift in perspective that a tunnel or fire can only approximate.

Results of psi experiments with pictures and my spontaneous dreams let me discover how easy it is to detect fire via our psi senses, no matter how far away the situation may be. Like fire, most highly energetic activities are good psi targets. Sometimes energetic targets are perceived as something less energetic or even emotionally neutral. For example, in the *Volcano* experiment, participants did not directly perceive the volcano but instead sensed a less threatening dynamic, such as a steam engine or fireworks. Regardless of how the energy or emotion of a target is subconsciously disguised, it remains highly visible in psi space—only the form is altered.

What can be done with this knowledge? Certainly, psi target pools could be constructed that are easier to sense and could thereby help contribute to scientifically proving the reality of psi phenomenon—a continuing concern of psi researchers. What about psi applications? I pondered this question frequently during the early days of my STARGATE involvement.

φ φ φ

As we approached the end of that first year of the remote viewing research contract with the Stanford Research Institute (SRI), I suspected that our results, though impressive from a research viewpoint, were not sufficiently compelling for contract renewal. The goalposts had been moved back, and review officials in my place of employment—Wright Patterson Air Force Base, Foreign Technology Division (FTD) in Dayton, Ohio—were asking questions that were not part of the initial research effort. Instead of acknowledging how successful our SRI remote viewing projects were in demonstrating that remote viewing is real, our Command people wanted to know what could be done with the phenomenon in a military setting. Only one year into a research program, the stakes were suddenly elevated. I knew that a contract technicality—that application demonstration was not part of the legal statement-of-work—would not win the day. Command's "event horizon" had suddenly shrunk.

I suspected they were feeling pressure from a contract review group in the Pentagon. The remote viewing research effort I had established in 1976 must certainly be unusual and therefore subject to more scrutiny than any other Air Force contract.

I felt this research was important and could lead to applications for search and rescue or for providing tip-offs on Soviet activities. What could be done in a few weeks to keep this innovative activity from being canceled? The more I brooded over this situation, the more impossible contract renewal seemed.

As I reminisce back to that time in 1977, I recall the intense soul searching I experienced during those days and nights. I was in an incredible dilemma. Here was the chance of a lifetime, a chance to fulfill a dream—albeit a dream I did not fully understand. But that chance seemed to be vanishing. I was caught between something unknown that was surging from deep within, urging me to continue this activity and the reality of overwhelming practical and political circumstances.

We then lived in Beavercreek, Ohio, and I often strolled in the forest near Beavercreek High School during that traumatic time, wondering what could be done, if anything. About two weeks prior to decision time when I would have to pass the word to have "pink slips" sent to the SRI remote viewing staff, I found myself idly strolling along the Little Miami River.

Suddenly, light images flashed from the river—like sunlight breaking through a cloud layer. As I pondered that "light flash," a startling idea came to me. Why not have the SRI remote viewers detect a U.S. rocket motor test? Certainly that would be a high-flash event, and I had seen enough evidence of psi's ability to detect the "power of fire." Detecting a rocket motor ignition would certainly resonate with Air Force interests. The implications would be exceedingly clear: If SRI remote viewers could sense a U.S. rocket motor test, they had the potential to sense a Soviet rocket motor test—or any other type of Soviet energetic test—even nuclear. This would be especially significant if our then-emergent spy satellites were also looking at the same rocket test and could not detect it. That was wild thinking! But . . . why not?

A few days later, I learned that a spy satellite test was planned, to see if it could detect a U.S. rocket motor test event in the Utah desert. I quickly made arrangements with SRI researchers to set up the necessary protocol so that we could also "take a look."

We set up a procedure that would eliminate possible anticipation of an event as a target. Hal had purposefully offset the laboratory clocks by five minutes to avoid potential criticism that an event had been guessed at, which would have occurred at an even hour or half hour. The only request given to the remote viewers was to "describe the target area" at coordinates XYZ. (In those days, we were using actual earth coordinates as "targeting techniques." Later we found this was not necessary.) In this case, even had remote viewers looked at a map, specific details of a test layout would not have been possible to determine—that information was only available from classified maps or classified photographs. Targeting procedures thus far implied that an area description was called for. Events had not previously been a project objective.

I was able to develop direct links with those who were monitoring the test. They were connected with the satellite system, and would be among the first to know if sensors on the satellite had seen anything. Very few people knew about this odd competition—remote viewers versus sophisticated satellite.

I had arranged to be "blind to" the results for at least one hour following the scheduled test. I did not want my knowledge to be a potential confounding parameter. I called my technology contact in the desert. "OK, Bill," I asked offhandedly, "how did the test go?"

He was quiet for a few seconds. "Well," he said disappointedly, "there has been a problem. The test did not go as planned. They will try again tomorrow."

I thanked him for the input and quickly called Hal Puthoff. "Hal," I remarked casually, "what did the remote viewers describe?" Anxiously, I awaited his response.

"Nothing unusual was sensed by either Hella Hammid or Ingo Swann (the two remote viewers for this project). "All they perceived was a *quiet, desert-like area*," he said calmly.

"Great!" I exclaimed. "The test was delayed; nothing happened. It has been rescheduled for tomorrow morning."

Hal seemed relieved. At least the remote viewers had not conjured up lots of activity when nothing had happened.

We rescheduled for the next day. Hella and Ingo remained in California, 500 miles from the test area in Utah. The second rocket ignition test was also delayed—again Hella and Ingo did not sense anything unusual. This is how the planned rocket test proceeded: one cancellation after another. The remote viewers held to their perceptions of a *calm, peaceful desert scene*. I am sure they were becoming puzzled as to why we were interested in a bland desert area. Then came the fourth scheduled test.

An hour after the planned event, I called my contact. "Hey, it blew!" shouted Bill. "It blasted at three seconds after the scheduled time this morning! It worked perfectly. What a sight!" He went on to describe the intense surge of exhaust fire that erupted from the rocket motor nozzle and the ear-shattering rumble that shook the desert landscape.

I did not know that this huge solid propellent rocket motor was housed above a thick concrete trough that would duct exhaust parallel to the ground. At ignition, hundreds of thousands of gallons of water were sprayed into the hot exhaust to keep surrounding structures cool. Exhaust flame and superheated steam surged through the trough and then curved upward, creating a spectacular white turbulent column that billowed high into the clear desert sky. This was, indeed, a powerful energetic event!

The rocket motor had ignited as intended and had shattered the silence of the desert. But had anyone distant—those who analyzed signals from the infrared sensors on the satellite high in the sky or the remote viewers 500 miles away in California—been able to detect the powerful blast? I called Hal and quietly waited for his response.

"OK," he said excitedly, "I guess the moment of truth is at hand. This time, our remote viewers had a reaction—and it was powerful! I have not observed such a response in any previous remote viewing experiments."

"Well, Hal," I asked casually, "what exactly did they perceive?"

"Hella was the most dramatic," he replied. "She said that something suddenly erupted, like *locomotive-powered steam*, and she drew a sketch of a *horizontal trough that ducts swirling flame and steam*.

Ingo perceived *a tall column of smoke rising into the sky.* They both checked the clock and noted the exact time. After I corrected their recordings to real time, I discovered that their impressions occurred about five seconds after 9:00 A.M. "

I listened quietly, absorbing information I found hard to believe. I thanked him for his call, asked him to Express Mail the remote viewers' data, and told him I would give feedback after I had received his package.

The next day, as I reviewed their sketches, it was obvious that Hella's and Ingo's data correlated very well with the actual test area configurations. Ingo had a general sketch of the area with a rising plume. Hella had drawn a very accurate sketch of the test stand structures that contained the path of the surging exhaust. They had sensed this event within a few seconds of its occurrence. With their responses in hand, I called Hal.

"Hal . . . thanks. I think you and your remote viewers have saved the program! Congratulations!" We talked awhile, envisioning new directions for remote viewing research.

Maybe my reaction was premature, but I doubted it. In a few days my technology contact called with interesting news—the high-tech satellite in the sky had not detected anything. The remote viewers had won that round.

After I had all the remote viewing and satellite information in hand, I made my case for continuing the remote viewing research program. My presentation occurred only days before the contractual cutoff cycle.

The response to the data I presented was essentially silence. The data spoke for itself; all present could now see the potential of remote viewing for detecting remote energetic events. Identifying emerging weapon system developments in the Soviet Union, via remote viewing, was a possibility.

A few days later, I was informed that the contract would be renewed. Hal, Hella and Ingo had won out.

Another tumultuous year of remote viewing research could now begin. I called Hal to give him the news. "Hal, are you ready for another year of remote viewing research?" I asked casually.

"Of course," Hal remarked dryly. "Any time you have a challenge like *West Test*, give us a call."

Over the years, I gave Hal and others on the remote viewing team many challenging calls as we continued our STARGATE odyssey.

I often muse over the events leading up to this *West Test* remote viewing experiment. There was more here than a long-distance remote viewing project. Without that timely window of opportunity, Hal's careful protocol, and the right desire and motivation from Ingo and Hella, remote viewing research in the Department of Defense would have folded in 1977, and there would not have been a STARGATE program. Arguments may go on for a long time debating the significance of STARGATE. Critics will certainly weigh in on the negative side. Eventually, however, *West Test* and other remote viewing activities will be seen as markers, as milestones in the evolution of our understanding of reality. Like beacons flashing in the night, such markers help us navigate deeper into the psychic domain where we can better perceive the nature of our interconnectivity with others and our environment. Psi data can help us know the truth and let us be better prepared for surprises around the corner.

φ φ φ

The *Psychic Realm* class experiences had given me an understanding of how people viewed the nature of psi and how psi can be of practical use. Class members had no difficulty accepting the help from their psi talents for their personal lives, such as finding lost items or being forewarned of an emerging situation. Many of them had impressive psi experiences, and our discussions served as a forum for experience sharing. Class members could readily see the potential for applying psi in police work, such as locating missing people or providing clues for solving crimes. I found it interesting that there was a general reluctance to perceive of psi as something of use to government organizations, especially those connected with intelligence activities. I did not do any surveys, but I could tell from occasional comments that most people harbored a negative feeling about applying psi phenomena to intelligence issues.

Even though I found this view puzzling, I could see why the general public might feel that way. Some government organizations had a less than positive image due to mishandling of important activities. Old stereotypes of incompetent bureaucrats lingered in people's perceptions. There was also a concern that by using psi, "Big Brother" could come to know all their secrets. Unfortunately, some science fiction stories helped propagate such notions. Some people felt that psi was more of a "sacred" experience than a "profane" one—so why mix metaphysics with a secular (government) activity? Although reasons varied for the negative views on potential government use of psi, there was one perception that seemed common to most, and that had to do with the question: What is the purpose of government intelligence activities? I came to understand that most of the concerns were due to varied opinions on the basic purpose of intelligence. The "cloak and dagger" image from WW II and the early Cold War days as portrayed in the media was generally less than wholesome.

Psi abilities have been applied for military purposes throughout history. I consider Jeanne d'Orléans—Joan of Arc—as the most famous historical military personage who used psi ability, or remote viewing, as she did for the French Army in the early 1400s. Her psi-like precognition of the "battle of the Herrings" between the French and British was accurate. She correctly predicted the winning strategy at the siege of Orléans and had other psi impressions that proved to be true. The origin of her data was interpreted in the context of the times. Initially, her impressions or imagery (visions) were seen as coming from a divine source. Later, they were seen as being from an evil source, which justified her execution at a burning stake.

I continued to ponder the question "Why intelligence activities?" Of course, I came to reconcile any potential dilemma —otherwise I would not have left a technical career with space programs and joined a government intelligence organization.

In principle, the fundamental purpose of intelligence is to know the truth, to be forewarned of imminent threats. Of course, there are complicating issues: Is the intelligence information always applied properly? Who sets policy and for what overall objective? Simply seeking to "know the truth" to avoid technical or political surprises may be noble, but whose truth is the truth? I suspected that the Soviet Union's intelligence operatives had their own version of deeply believed truth. This question may be similar to "Whose religion has the truth?"

I opted for the "higher reason"—that intelligence activities are for knowing the truth and by implication for helping us respond appropriately to avoid global war. Since the nuclear powers were poised at the brink of nuclear exchange, anything that could help avoid such a catastrophe should be sought. I could only hope the ideology within any political system—capitalism, communism or other forms—would be responsive to the "higher reason" that peace and freedom are the objectives. In practice, deviations from such ideals occur. It is the nature of the human situation, especially if a nation's survival as a social, political or economic system is perceived to be threatened.

Even with a philosophical acceptance of this higher goal, I still remained bothered. Who can really judge what is best for an individual or a nation? Can we deceive ourselves and miss the big picture or fail to see the long-term consequences of inappropriate near-term acts? Emphasis on near-term gain (quarterly profits) and the "now" mentality that dominates our culture did not seem conducive to good long-term decision making.

I eventually took the view that I could not really know what would be best from a long-term perspective. All I could do was hope that keeping overall guiding principles in mind, such as "avoiding war, promoting peace," would help sort out the specifics—those I could choose and those chosen by national leaders.

This philosophizing was relevant to my pursuit of psi and its potential applications. Specifically, how could I really know if psi should be sought as a potential intelligence application? As I mused over what was emerging as a major dilemma, I had several unusual symbolic and realistic dreams that seemed relevant. They were brief, and offered encouragement for continuing my explorations, not only for the study of psi phenomena, but also for the investigation of psi intelligence-gathering potential.

> *I am in a field and see a target of concentric circular areas in the distance. I know it is too far away to hit. Suddenly I throw a dart high into the air and watch it fall directly into the center. Somehow, I had hit the target!*

> *I am in an airplane looking through a lens. It has the capability to bring anything into focus, no matter how far away. I turn the lens and see the ground zoom up toward me. I keep turning and can see into a building.*

These dreams occurred when I was troubled about the reality of psi, how to explain it, and how to know the limits of its potential applications. They had a clear message: Do not be concerned about the mechanism of psi or how to explain it—simply set the goal, and the information will come into focus. However, I remained concerned about applying psi for intelligence. I suspected that my excursions into psi had brought me close to an aspect of myself that is universal. I was not into metaphysics or New Age thinking; however, I could not deny that psi implied the existence of something beyond ourselves. But what? A "principle" like gravity or something like a collective unconscious or a collective mind? If a collective mind existed, then could larger decisions or judgments occur in that domain—perhaps for integrating everything that was happening or intended? Would such decisions not be for an overall constructive goal for our species as a whole, including our planet and our environment? Sigmund Freud's "censor" and Carl Jung's idea of wholeness suggested that an integrating principle existed at subconscious levels that had individual and collective long-term perspectives.

My willingness to plunge into psi research and intelligence applications was driven by the hope that the higher goal of "avoiding war by knowing the truth" was the most fundamental aspect of intelligence, and that, somehow, a subconscious interconnecting principle would eventually nudge our various paths as individuals or nations toward a positive evolutionary progression.

I surmised that only psi information that was constructive could be accessed via psi. Otherwise, attempts for psi access would fail and that information could not be known. Even the best psi sensitive would not succeed.

During this period of intense "soul and goal" searching, I experienced a vivid dream that related to these concerns:

> *I am in a remote area walking along a dark road. Directly ahead,*
> *I notice a barbed wire fence. A brightly lit building blocks the*
> *road. As I approach, a guard shouts at me in a foreign language*
> *that I recognize as Russian. Then he begins to speak English*
> *and asks me why I am here. I explain that I am exploring and*
> *am interested in knowing what is within the guarded zone. The*
> *guard objects violently and forbids me to enter. I ask him to call*
> *his supervisor and consult with him. After a brief hesitation, he*

*picks up a telephone and calls someone. When the conversation
ends, he turns to me and reluctantly says, "OK . . . you can
enter."*

*I notice a lake or bay, but it is dark and I cannot see clearly.
Suddenly, a light comes on, and I see a very large ship. I climb on
board. Someone whom I cannot clearly see shows me around. I
notice pipes, glass-like devices, and a large reflecting surface, like a
mirror, near the top of the ship. I observe this device and become
aware that I am in a dream. As I become lucid, I think about the
odd mirror device, trying to determine what it is for, and the
dream disappears. I am now aware of being in bed.*

I felt electrical sensations, usually an indication that a dream is of
psi origin.

The dream conveyed a sense of "penetrating a type of barrier." If
literal, then I had "visited," via a remote viewing dream, a secret facility
. . . maybe in the Soviet Union! I found it intriguing that a debate
occurred between the guard and me and then between the guard and
his supervisor for seeking access approval. This aspect of the dream
suggested that some type of subconscious decision process had
occurred. Could this indicate that, at some deep level, "secrets" may
not always be what we want them to be? The guard was guarding a
secret but then withdrew objections to my knowing what it was. The
ship in the dream was huge and could have been a large destroyer or
an aircraft carrier.

As I reviewed the dream, I felt a growing conviction that this was
not a symbolic dream of personal significance. I suspected that it did
represent something secret: a new and significant emerging Soviet
system—specifically, a high-energy, ship-based laser weapon! I could
rationalize no other reason for a *large mirror* or lots of *glass and
plumbing*. The idea of a *guarded facility* also suggested a new type of
system. Optical tracking was old technology and would not have to be

guarded. Even though I did not identify the objects as lasers or laser-related during the dream, I could see no other likely interpretation.

The specific type of system—a high-energy, ship-based laser—did not seem logical. All I could do was record the impression and see if such a system would eventually emerge.

Later that week, I met with intelligence analysts responsible for assessing laser technology. I did not mention the dream. When I queried about the likelihood of the Soviets developing a high-energy, ship-based laser, the response was emphatic: No way! The experts thought little of such a wild notion. Consequently, I did not discuss the idea with anyone, but I did not forget it, and I occasionally searched the available data on Soviet developments to see if anything like my ship-laser was anticipated. I found nothing, not even in long-range forecasts. Ground-based, high-energy lasers, yes; ship-based, no.

Six years after my *High-Energy Laser* dream, I came across a new assessment of Soviet developments that showed evidence for an emerging weapon system—a high-energy, ship-based laser.

I could at last put closure on that old dream. It was an "alert" dream; it did have information of an emerging system that had probably entered the early phases of development at the time of the dream. I could not be sure why I had that specific dream. Maybe the high-energy aspect, the powerful fire-like nature of such a device, helped bring it into my psi space excursions. Whatever caused it, it did help me to resolve a major inner conflict: The dream helped me "not to worry" about the potential use of psi. We could access the secrets of others—even nations—but only if those secrets could help achieve some higher objective. I was reasonably sure that avoiding a global holocaust, maintaining world peace, and—implicit for me—maintaining a democratic way of life with its personal freedom were more significant for global society in the long term than were the goals developed by a freedom-limiting ideology.

Perhaps the secret I accessed was similar in nature to those perceived by psi sensitives working on police cases. The criminal wants to hide the truth, but society wants it known. This leads to the question: What is private, what is secret? I suspect that certain types of information, including those we truly consider private, are not accessible via psychic means. Some types of "secrets" can become known, depending on subconscious awareness of long-term implications and how the information is to be used.

φ φ φ

I have seen repeatedly that energetic incidents are great beacons in psi space. Fire is especially bright for ordinary senses and for our psi scanning process. Even potential situations, such as those revealed by precognition of emerging fire or fire-like incidents, planned or accidental, loom intense to our psi process. Reluctance to report such incidents, or lack of a way to report them, minimizes our awareness of them. But could that not change? Why cannot more people acknowledge such experiences? With a growing awareness of psi's potential for anyone, more people could be on the alert for emerging fire-threat situations, especially those significant for their own well-being or the safety of others. Pioneer researcher Dr. Louise E. Rhine believed that psi could be applied in this way. In *Hidden Channels of the Mind* (1961, page 189), she wrote: "If precognition ability is developed and directed, as in time it is reasonable to expect it will be, its operation, even on a limited basis, could obviously be of untold value to humanity."

Precognition or future-seeing has the potential for preventing tragedies like the bombing of the Alfred P. Murrah Federal Building in Oklahoma City. I suspect that many people who worked in that building had relevant premonitions, perhaps hunches or dreams of fire.

With no way to explore the significance of their dreams, especially in a society that still disregards dreams, what could they really do? I also suspect that a few people felt sick but went to the office anyway. During the heart-rending interviews that affected all of us in the days after that act of terrorism in 1995, I only heard one reference to a premonition. A woman told the television interviewer that her husband felt uneasy that morning due to a terrifying dream. They did not explore the dream, and he rushed away to get to the office on time.

With no experience in working with their latent psi talent, I suspect that many people blocked the knowledge—the truth—that was approaching them. No one should block such knowledge, and we do not need to. But we must overcome self-imposed barriers. Then we can—as Dr. Rhine envisioned—take that next step in evolution, a step that acknowledges our interconnectivity with others and with our future. This is not a useless link; it has life-saving potential.

chapter three

Airplane Down

φ

I have described many examples of how intensely energetic events such as fires or explosions are like bright beacons to our psi sensitivities. The physical and psychological trauma from airplane crashes can also generate intense emotional signals in the domain of psi.

Various reasons exist for why some missing airplane searches are unsuccessful; the emergency location equipment may have either malfunctioned, or the signal was obscured by terrain features. Data from psi sources could provide information on terrain features and landmarks to help locate or narrow down search options. Psi data can also assist in locating missing children, prisoners of war and hostages.

Evidence from psi research and application projects has indicated that emotional connection with a missing individual improves the quality of the psi data. Some psi sensitives avoid emotional connectivity, but most feel that this is important. If the missing person is not known to the psi sensitive, he or she usually requires some means to establish connectivity, such as studying his or her name, observing the missing person's photograph, or holding something of value to that person. Those who prefer a structured approach to psi via specific remote viewing techniques do not consider that rapport with others is important for search application. I suspect this perspective has to do with avoidance of anything suggesting that the psi process involves mind-to-mind connectivity with a possible telepathic aspect. *Telepathy* is a term coined in the late 1800s to categorize some psi experiences. It was based on the concept that an electromagnetic signal is sent by the distant person and received by the psi sensitive. Experiments[6] have shown that psi is independent of electromagnetic propagation. Initially, telepathy referred to detecting feeling states or emotions in the other person, but current psi researchers use the term *telepathy* to include any type of knowledge, not only feeling states.

After exploring and carefully evaluating the data—both research and actual search efforts—I accepted psi's potential for locating missing people and missing airplanes. But how accurate could the data be, and how could it be factored in with information from conventional sources?

The remote viewing research provided great insight on data accuracy. There were many examples where key features in the target area were identified correctly. Gary Langford sketched *a large circular building with a white dome*. He said it reminded him of a huge flying saucer in the middle of a city. The target was the Louisiana Superdome, 3,000 miles away. Hella Hammid drew a sketch of a *diagonal trough up in the air* that correlated with a pedestrian overpass target a few miles away. In another target, she described *underground caves or mines . . . deep shafts . . . cool . . . moist, earth-smelling passages*. The target was the Ohio Caverns.[7] *Psychic Realm* participants produced accurate descriptions of places in the Dayton, Ohio area that I had chosen as remote viewing targets. These, and many other examples, illustrated that remote viewing can help narrow down search possibilities, detect key terrain features with sufficient accuracy to guide a search team, or even lead to the exact location of a missing airplane or person.

Psi sensitives have been involved in searches for missing airplanes. Harold Sherman accurately described the area where a missing private plane was eventually found in a mountain area in the state of Washington. Shirley Harrison, a psi sensitive from Maine, had a good track record in a variety of psi applications, including locating missing people, objects and airplanes. In one search project, her information led to the location of an airplane in New Hampshire that had been missing for several months.[8]

It became clear to me that psi sensitives could make a major contribution to almost any search project, especially when the terrain is variable with clear reference points. Some locations, however, such as deep in a jungle or a vast desert might pose difficulty. Psi data, as I had discovered, are not to scale and can be inaccurate in distance and size. Ten miles might seem like only a couple of miles to a psi sensitive. A large mountain or lake may seem to be only a ridge and pond. Even with scaling difficulties, psi data can still provide assistance, especially if the search has been ongoing with no success. Encouraged by remote viewing successes, I developed search procedures to use should an opportunity occur. I was fortunate at that time to have discovered a psi-talented individual, Diane, from my organization who shared my enthusiasm for finding things. Our remote viewing and psi dream work—in Chapter 1—provided convincing evidence of her ability to provide meaningful psi data in real search missions. What could such a mission be?

φ φ φ

When I was suddenly called into an unexpected meeting, I knew that something "big" was going on. I could not imagine what it could be. There had been no rumors of anything unusual, no major reorganization, and no intriguing project. There were only a few senior military officers present.

I took a seat at the side of the room and waited for them to speak. Someone closed the door and locked it. My interest was piqued, especially when all present turned toward me! What had I done?

After a few moments of silence, the ranking official spoke. "I suppose you are wondering why you have been asked to this meeting." I glanced at him and remained quiet. He got to the point. "We heard about your quiet little project," he said sternly.

I was not sure which one he meant. All I could do was mutter, "Oh" and wait for him to continue.

"Let me say this up front. We do not know if what you are into is real or not. But if there is anything at all to this . . . uh . . . this remote viewing . . . then we are now giving you an opportunity to prove it."

I was surprised. What did he mean? Only a few people knew about my remote viewing contract with SRI. I knew that proving the phenomenon with statistical means required lots of data . . . and years of work. How could I be called upon to prove it now? I explained our research and how we were only beginning to get into proof-of-principle projects. He did not allow me to complete my rationale.

"No, no, we do not mean to prove it in that sense. What about that Air Force person you are working with? We heard about how she has described distant scenes quite accurately."

I wondered how they knew that. "Yes," I quickly replied. "Her data has surprised me; she is very accurate. But we have only done a few of those, and they were not for scientific proof."

"We know that," he interrupted. "Do you think she can describe the location of a missing airplane accurately enough so that we can find it?"

Now I understood. A real search project was in progress. This was exactly what Diane and I had been waiting for! I wondered why I had not read about an Air Force missing plane or picked up any rumor of it.

"How soon can you start?" he asked tersely.

"Anytime. But I do need to get approval so that Diane and I do not run into conflicts with our routine assignments," I said casually.

"You both already have approval. We have taken care of that minor administrative detail."

"Oh."

"By the way," he quickly informed me, "this entire effort is highly guarded . . . your part of it especially so. I think you can understand that."

I certainly could. Using remote viewing to help in an Air Force search project could cause problems if our involvement leaked to the press.

We discussed the protocol that I envisioned for search projects and they agreed to my approach. I would have Diane attempt to describe the missing airplane's location, via remote viewing, in two phases. In Phase One, she would be shown a picture of the airplane type. If her perceptions correlated with anything recognizable in the suspected search area, then I would go to the second phase. In Phase Two she would attempt to perceive additional terrain details in the crash site area and then examine topographic maps to see if she could pinpoint where the plane could be found. I felt that this two-step approach would minimize any expectations or biases on her part that might distort her remote viewing impressions. After agreeing on procedures, the official opened an envelope and gave me the photo of the missing airplane that they were so anxious to locate. I gazed at it in disbelief. It was a Soviet airplane! Now I understood why there had been no publicity in the media.

"We are able to narrow the area where we believe the airplane to have crashed to about 40,000 to 50,000 square miles," the officer explained. "We will withhold that information from you until after your source has completed the first phase. But we think you should tell her at least the continent. We do not have a lot of time left in this search effort before the Soviets, or some other country, find the airplane before we do."

Now I was even more intrigued. "You see," he continued, "here is your challenge. That Soviet-built airplane is missing somewhere in Africa! That is a huge place. It could be buried deep in desert sands or smothered in a dense jungle, in some other terrain, or even out at sea. We do not know. We have an opportunity to recover it—and analyze it—if only we can find it. I want to emphasize that other countries that know it is missing are searching as desperately as we. We believe that we have a slight advantage over them, since we have reports of its last known sighting."

I had never expected a real search project to be easy—but anywhere in or near Africa? Why could we not have been brought into an easy one, like an airplane missing in the Rockies, or in Ohio? But now was not the time to waffle. Opportunities such as this were not likely to come again soon. It was time to put remote viewing on the line. Isn't that what I had been saying? If psi is not useful for anything, why bother with it?

I placed the airplane photograph in the thick envelope and headed for the door. "Thanks," I said. "This will be interesting. I will be in contact later today."

I unlocked the door and stepped out into the busy hallway—to find Diane and give her the good news! When I explained the challenge I had accepted, however, she had quite a different perception of what was meant by good news.

"You . . . what! Locate a missing Soviet airplane . . . in . . . Africa? Are you kidding, or . . . what?"

"No, Diane," I interrupted, "this is not a joke. I am serious. This is a crucial project. It is very important that the search team finds the airplane, very soon. There may be only a few days left before. . . ."

"Oh, I see," she replied, nodding slowly, and gazing at something on or beyond my office wall. I waited for her to continue.

"OK, this is what we have been working toward," she said confidently. "So, what are we waiting for?"

I sensed that she was feeling something like that first time you walk to the edge of the high diving board and look down into the pool. Sometimes it is best not to think too much about a new venture. Set your goal; go at it with confidence, determined to succeed. Then do it!

"Let's go for it now, Diane."

It was 5:00 P.M. and the office was empty for the day. She agreed with the two-phase approach—go for impressions first and then examine the topographic map of the suspected search zone.

"All I know is the airplane is a Soviet-built bomber. Here is a picture of what it looks like." I handed her the photograph. She glanced at it, held it for a few moments, and placed it on the table.

My procedure for remote viewing projects was straightforward. I explained the task and occasionally reminded the remote viewer about the objective. The remote viewer, after a brief relaxing period, would wait patiently for impressions and sketch them or describe them verbally. In Diane's previous remote viewing experiments with targets in the Dayton area she had worked alone most of the time and needed no one to keep her focused on the goal. I was well aware that anyone present during a remote viewing session must have no knowledge of the target to avoid potential subliminal cuing. I did not know the suspected search area—and no one knew the airplane's location.

After a few minutes of relaxing to turn her focus of attention inward, she glanced up and said, "OK, I am ready."

"Diane," I began slowly, "an airplane is missing like the one in this photograph; describe its location . . . describe the location of the missing airplane. . . ." I paused and waited.

Some remote viewers preferred to have a monitor or interviewer present during the remote viewing session to help them occasionally refocus on the task. Having someone else pose the task minimizes the analytical thinking that can interfere with the remote viewing process and lead to premature analysis of the emerging impressions. Diane did not need to be reminded of the objective. After initiating the session, my role was that of a passive observer. As I sat quietly across the table from her, I felt that my intentions for her to succeed might be of help. I could not be sure, but I felt that adding positive thoughts could assist her remote viewing process. So I sat quietly, eyes closed, intending her to achieve success.

After fifteen or twenty minutes of silence, I could hear that she was sketching. I opened my eyes and saw that she was drawing terrain features. When she finished the sketch, she paused briefly and then drew a curving line over the markings she had made on the plain white paper. Then she glanced up at me.

"I think this is all I am going to get right now," she said slowly. "I did have a scene flash as I relaxed . . . like a panoramic view. I even saw huge mountains and large lakes . . . I felt the plane had traveled . . . this way." She gave her sketch to me and pointed to the airplane path.

I was surprised at the details. It would be easy to tell whether she was way off or had actually described features in the search area. Even if her sketch matched a portion of the search zone, however, was it accurate enough for finding the plane? As I studied her sketch, she began talking about the airplane from a perspective inside the plane's cockpit. It was as if she was reliving what the pilot saw and felt during the last moments of the plane's flight. Then she abruptly stopped talking.

"That is it. Can't do anymore. I am not sure what happened to the pilot. . . . He may have bailed out. . . . He may not know where the plane went. . . ."

"Diane, you seem to have made contact with the target area," I said enthusiastically. "I have the feeling that your sketches will make sense to the search team. I will pass it to them as soon as I xerox what you have drawn. Thanks. Thank you very much."

About an hour had passed since the remote viewing session had begun, and she had to leave. I remained to write a few notes for the file I was developing. After xeroxing her sketch and my notes, I went to the room where the search team was sequestered and handed the sketch to the official I had met earlier.

He glanced at the sketch. "Thanks," he said, showing no emotion. "We will take a look at this and let you know . . . probably tomorrow morning." I knew this was a round-the-clock operation and that they had direct links to the search team in Africa.

I drove home lost in thought, my analytical nature in high gear. Diane's sketch had unique features that should be easy to identify. When I arrived home, I located a *National Geographic* map of Africa. One region had the features she had sketched. I knew that she would be either way off the target—or right on target. Still, the big question: Was her sketch accurate enough in scale for the search effort? And even if she had perceived the search area, had she sensed it from the subconscious of search team members through telepathy, or was it from the remote place?

I had wrestled with the question of psi data source ever since becoming involved in remote viewing research. It was easy to make assumptions about how psi worked, but no one knew. The best procedure was to defer the data source question and look at the data for source inferences. Sometimes another person's knowledge did seem important. In double-blind experiments, where no one knew the target, the psi process still worked. Diane had shown the ability to access knowledge held in mind by someone and also to access information in concealed envelopes, unknown to anyone. All I could do was wait and hold onto the concept that she had "gone to the truth" and not to someone's expectation or preconceived ideas.

I arrived at the office early the next day. The phone was ringing; it was my search team contact. "Please come to my office now," he said tersely. "We need to talk." Quickly, I walked to his office area. The moment of truth had arrived.

"Are you sure you—or your source—have not seen our search area map?"

I objected emphatically, "No! How could we? Why?"

"Then it is time to show you the search area . . . and move to your second phase. Come into this room and take a look," he said excitedly.

We walked into a secure area, and I gazed at the maps on the wall. They showed a large portion of a jungle area. "Let me show you something," he said, as he picked up a large pointer. "We have been focusing here . . ." He pointed to a small area on the top portion of the search zone. "This is the region where people on the ground reported booming or crashing sounds around the time the plane was sighted. So, naturally, we expect it to be here. That is where we are searching. This larger area of 40,000 square miles is based on various calculations of where it might have flown. So you see, what is interesting is this: Your source's sketch has features that can be found in the larger area, and the airplane path that she put on her sketch is not near where we are looking."

I could see why he was excited. If the search team had no success in the smaller area using locational equipment and searchers on the ground, then maybe the problem was just that they were looking in the wrong place. I was now sure of one important aspect: Diane had not sensed the search team's expectations. She had very likely accessed "the truth."

"I think it is time," he said enthusiastically, "to go to Phase Two— now!"

He gave me a copy of the search area maps, and I quickly sought Diane. Now was the time for her to study the maps to see if she could narrow down the impact area of that airplane. When I rolled open the maps, she immediately exclaimed, "That's it! That is the scene I saw."

"OK, you are on track," I responded quietly. "Based on the scene you saw and your sketch, circle the area on the map where you think the plane is located."

I sat very still, watching her study the maps. "Here . . ." she said, after a few moments. "I am sure this is the area." She drew a circle on one of the maps and handed it to me. The spot she had marked was at least sixty miles away from the suspected crash location.

"Thanks, Diane. This should help the search team. We will see what happens."

I called my search contact, introduced him to Diane, and gave him the map she had marked. I knew he would send the information directly to the search team in the field, but could they use it? I knew time was running out and hoped that the search team could take a quick-look fly-over. All we could do was wait.

I had also contacted Dr. Hal Puthoff at SRI and made arrangements to work with one of their remote viewers. I made a quick trip to SRI and served as the interviewer for Gary Langford. He perceived the plane to have crashed into a steep ridge with small reddish streams nearby. Maybe his impressions would narrow possibilities within the area indicated by Diane.

While I was at SRI, the search team received a response from the field. They were highly interested in the data from Diane. She was contacted again and asked to mark the exact crash site within the area she had circled. She reexamined the map and placed an "X" within the circle. The coordinate of the "X" was transmitted to the field.

We waited.

Two days later we were called into the search operations office. I could feel the electricity in the air. Something had happened, but what?

"The airplane has been found," my contact said excitedly, "and just in the nick of time! We only had one more day before calling off the search."

"Where was it?" I asked casually.

He turned toward Diane. "It was within three miles of your X," he said enthusiastically.

Diane and I were speechless.

"When we received your information," he continued, "we began to shift the search to the region that Diane indicated. Our pilots were alerted, and they began flying around in that general area. Some of our field team members began traveling to that location. We put out information to natives in the region to be on the lookout for signs of a crash, and then . . . a native did come to us with a metal fragment. It was from the Soviet airplane."

"Even though the military searchers did not find the plane," he continued, "we know that shifting focus to the area marked by Diane led to the discovery of the plane. We are confident that our reconnaissance planes would eventually have found the plane, based on your data. Fragments of the plane—and the swath it made through the trees—were visible from low-flying aircraft."

The plane had crashed into the side of a steep ridge, as Gary had sketched. Red-tinted streams flowed from the ridge. Regardless of how the plane was actually found, one simple fact remained: Out of a 40,000 square mile area, Diane had pinpointed the crash site to within three miles. This was especially significant since the search team had been convinced it was sixty miles away. Diane's mark on the topographic map was based purely on visual impressions that matched the topography of the crash area. There was no guessing involved. A thorough check of all message dates proved conclusively that our data had been received in the field at least two days before the plane was found.

I thought our involvement with this search project would become part of the classified files and be forgotten. We had no official role in locating the plane, and only a few people knew of our involvement. But I was satisfied that Diane and I had demonstrated the potential of remote viewing in search missions. Six years later, I had a chance to talk with the chief of the field search team. He said that his team would have found the airplane based on Diane's data. Former President Carter spoke of our search project and credited a "psychic source" as pinpointing the plane's location.

At that time I was unaware of the interest this project would generate in the media and the political scene in Washington, DC. Even though our involvement in the airplane search project was guarded, it somehow leaked to the press. Unbeknownst to me, a trial-by-fire period had begun due to a sensationalist article in the *Washington Post*.

Suddenly, we were no longer a small exploratory activity. It quickly became common knowledge in the military and other government areas that "the Air Force had used psychics to help locate a missing Soviet airplane." The association to the "psychic" image was something we had worked hard to avoid. The term "psychic" had too much unfortunate baggage and was generally associated with trickery and charlatans. We knew from our remote viewing work that not all professional psychics are frauds but "image" and "perception" can be significant—especially in Washington, DC.

Now the "naysayers" spoke out. Unfortunately, some were in positions of scientific authority. "Psi is impossible," claimed several chief scientists in the Department of Defense. Then came those who claimed to be on the side of the religious truth. "They are in cahoots with something demonic," they exclaimed. I could not believe this reaction. All we were trying to do—and did accomplish—was to determine the location of a missing airplane.

Without warning, I was thrust into chaos. I gave many briefings to review officials. Reporters started nibbling and speculative stories started erupting. It was easy to sense our FTD Commander's growing uneasiness with this unwanted visibility. We retreated from this controversy as best we could. It was clear that this was not the time to be open about psi. Earlier, we had considered sponsoring open research, but that idea was now squelched. Back to closed-door activity—and even that might not be feasible.

Then in the midst of the tension created by those news media leaks, we were brought into another search project. I was not sure if we should participate, but the pull to see how psi can help in search projects was too strong. This time we set up very tight controls on who would know of our remote viewing project.

The task was to locate a missing U.S. Air Force plane. I alerted Diane and Gary Langford at SRI. The only information I was given was a photograph of the airplane type. I was not told where it might be, or even on what continent, and I did not want to know. Only if our data matched the general search area would we continue to the map-marking phase. Nothing had been in the media about an Air Force search effort.

I worked with Diane at our facility; Dr. Puthoff worked with Gary at SRI. Diane's and Gary's impressions were consistent with terrain typical of a Southwest desert area. I passed this information to the search team contact. He then informed us that the airplane was missing in New Mexico and asked us to proceed with the map phase. I was reasonably sure we were on track.

When I laid out a large topographical map of New Mexico, Diane seemed perplexed. After a few minutes of concentration, her gaze shifted to El Capitan, a tall mountain in the southern part of New Mexico. She placed an X on the southeastern side, about two-thirds up the slope and drew a one-quarter-mile circle around the X.

"Something is wrong," she said cautiously. "I am torn between a flat desert area and this peak. There is something of interest, here, but I am not sure what. Anyway, this is what I sense." I was not sure how to interpret her confusion, and I presented both possibilities to my search team contact.

"Hate to tell you," he said firmly, "we have searched every square inch of that mountain. I can assure you the plane is not there. And those desert sketches . . . we need a specific place in the desert. You need to go back to your sources and try again. Look for a reference point that we can pass on to the search pilots."

I agreed to schedule another remote viewing session. "Time is running out," he said quickly. "The search may be called off in a day or two. If you can get anything more, I need it . . . today."

Diane and Gary were not available that day. Filled with disappointment, I found an empty conference room in which to ponder what to do, if anything. I felt uncomfortable with my own psi potential, especially for critical search activity where only psi sensitives with established track records should be involved. But . . . why not? I relaxed, hoping to "see the crash scene."

I am looking at a vast desert plain from low altitude. It is starkly divided into a white region and a black region. The black area has a slight rise and is separated from the white region by a low straight boundary like a black wall. In the center, near the boundary, I see two or three smoke-like columns rise straight up into the sky. They originate from holes. There are tall mountains nearby.

Startled, I quickly sketched this fleeting impression. At first I felt elated; maybe I had sensed something relevant. As I studied my sketch, I became less confident. Even if the scene was generally on track, I knew there were no such smoke sources in the desert. The sketch had no useful landmarks.

Later that day, I met with my contact. I suspected this would be our last meeting. "Well, did your sources come up with anything new?" he asked dryly.

"Yes, one of them did, but I do not understand it," I replied casually. I handed the sketch to him without telling him who the source was.

He gazed at it intently. "Hey, wait a minute!" he exclaimed. "This is interesting! What does your source think these black smoke columns are?"

I had the same question! "Don't know," I muttered. "Maybe they are symbolic of something . . . like markers, to call our attention to . . ." I did not finish. I was not even sure why I had said that.

"There is something I should tell you," he commented wryly. "There are two airplanes missing, not one. Maybe this sketch represents where they both crashed. We believe they came down close together."

"Two airplanes?"

"Yes, two. We did not want you to know that. We think their fuel systems malfunctioned during maneuvers, or maybe their gauges showed false readings and they ran out of fuel at the same time. If so, the planes must have gone straight down. The pilots had ejected but did not see what happened to the planes. If the planes went nose down, all that might be seen are hole-like depressions."

I was surprised to learn of two missing planes but could not see how my sketch was helpful.

"Have you ever been to this part of the desert?" he quizzed.

"No."

"Let me show you something," he said, as he pulled a photograph from a file drawer. "Take a look at this aerial photograph."

I studied it intently. There it was! There was the black boundary. I could hardly believe that the desert could have such a stark dividing line. To the north was a wide black area; to the south was the white of the white sands region. It looked as if a wall separated them.

"Maybe they are not far from the edge of this dark region in the Valley of Fire or the road that passes across it," he said emphatically.

I was enthused. Reassured at his interpretation of my sketch, I insisted that he also consider the data from Diane and Gary. He agreed to forward all the data to the field and called the search team. The next day they would take another look near the boundary of the black region and also at the mountain's southeast side, on their return. This would probably be the last day of the search.

I left his office knowing that we had done all we could. Even if my impressions were off track, at least they were the key for having Diane's and Gary's data examined. A lot was on the line. I do not recall sleeping much that night. All I could do was hope that in some way our data would be of help.

No one called the next day. Maybe the search mission had been scrubbed. Then, shortly after I arrived at the office the following day, the phone rang. It was my point-of-contact for the airplane search. "Hey, you will not believe this!" he shouted. "The helicopters did a fly-by over those areas yesterday, and they found a plane where your source had marked on the slope of El Capitan. It was within one-quarter mile of the X."

"What!"

"But . . ." he quickly added, "it was a different plane! It was a private plane that had been missing for several years. When the helicopter made a pass over the area near that map mark, they caught a glimpse of metal. They had looked there before but had not noticed it."

So . . . the highs and lows of search projects. I could tell he was as disappointed as I was. "What about the black boundary area?" I asked cautiously.

"They flew low and slow but noticed nothing unusual," he replied. "The planes may be further back from that boundary. That is a huge area. They have to be closer to the ground, or on it, to see any holes if the planes went nose-in."

I could sense his interest drifting. I felt the same way. We were close . . . but not close enough. Finding any plane, though gratifying, was not good enough.

The news media eventually carried stories on the official search and the lack of success. Fortunately, no one in the media picked up on our remote viewing involvement. At least we had had another opportunity to see what potential remote viewing had for airplane search projects. I felt reasonably satisfied that we had demonstrated a potential and hoped that we would have a chance to become involved in other missions. If we could keep at it long enough we would eventually learn how to better perform search projects and provide data accurate enough for defining more precise areas.

Several months after the search for the two Air Force planes was halted, I received a surprise call from my search team contact.

"Guess what?" he asked dryly.

"Don't tell me . . . don't tell me . . . I know. Someone on foot found the planes!"

"You got it! Remember that last sketch you gave to me?" How could I forget—it was my sketch! "I certainly do," I replied.

"Well, we should have pressed on with it," he said slowly. You see, a rancher found a funny crater. Nearby he noticed another crater. He began digging in one of them and found pieces of metal. No fragments were visible anywhere on the surface. Both of the planes had gone straight in and were buried."

I was not surprised. "Tell me," I asked intently, "were the two funny craters near that black boundary?"

"That they were!"

We had demonstrated that remote viewing can have a significant role in a variety of search projects. As a result of these search projects, my motivation for remote viewing research and applications became stronger than ever.

We did not have to wait long. When the Iran hostage crisis occurred in 1979, Diane and I were contacted by a ranking intelligence official in the Pentagon to see if we could provide data on the hostages, their exact location, and their physical and psychological situation. I also contacted Hal Puthoff to involve his remote viewers at SRI. Some of the remote viewing information did provide insight into the hostages status. In one instance, a remote viewer from SRI, Keith Harary, perceived that one of the hostages, Mr. Queen, would be released in two or three days for medical reasons. We alerted the National Security Council. Two days later, Mr. Queen was released unexpectedly due to a serious physical condition.

φ φ φ

A few months after the desert airplane search project, I received an invitation to apply for a prestigious intelligence community program that provided opportunities for working with private research organizations, universities and government laboratories. I felt the time was right to bring parapsychology—including remote viewing—out of the closet. I wrote a proposal for research with several parapsychological and biophysics facilities.

My project included developing statistical methods and researching cognitive processes, including electromagnetic effects on brain mechanisms. My proposal was approved through the initial evaluation processes and was one of the finalist contenders. In several weeks, word came from the office of the Director of Central Intelligence (DCI) that my proposal had been one of the those selected.

Then, a dramatic dream occurred:

I am flying a small experimental airplane at a high speed, low to the ground. The terrain zooms past. Suddenly, I see a high bridge and realize that I cannot pull up in time to fly over it. I keep going straight and pass under it. But directly ahead is a steel wall that extends high into the sky! I cannot avoid it and crash. I move through the barrier but know that my airplane has been destroyed.

I woke up, startled. The dream was too intense to ignore, and the symbolism was very clear. Something catastrophic was about to happen to me or to something I valued. I was sure the dream did not allude to anything physical—I had survived the crash. But what had crashed?

The dream required little analysis. It suggested that my DCI program was about to crash. Logically, that seemed impossible. The award had been approved by the director of the intelligence community. Who could overturn that decision?

There had been recent publicity on remote viewing that I was sure had left a negative image with policy makers. Unfortunately, someone supportive of remote viewing wrote a highly sensationalistic article that appeared in a military journal. I could see how those unfamiliar with the field might not find the article credible and assign "guilt by association" to all aspects of psi, even the solid research we were pursuing. I knew that our work on remote viewing was considered controversial by some, but it was also seen as innovative and forward-looking by others. So why that disturbing dream?

Weeks passed. Finally, the time arrived for traveling to Central Intelligence Agency (CIA) headquarters in Washington, DC, where I and a few others would officially receive our DCI program awards. Maybe I had misinterpreted that ominous dream.

Then, the phone call came. My research program had been withdrawn by the chief of staff of the Air Force. The caller provided no rationale as to why it was withdrawn.

I thanked him for the information. So . . . that dream was on track.

In the following weeks, my contacts in Washington tried every method they could to find out why the chief of staff had withdrawn my program. No direct reason was ever given; we could only speculate. After considering the pros and cons of a confrontation, we decided to wait a year and try again. A new person would be in his position by that time.

Some years later, an individual who had been on staff at the time and felt that he knew the reasons for the cancellation suggested that one reason was a deeply held fear or antagonism toward anything psi-related, perhaps from an uninformed scientific viewpoint. The other more likely reason was the MX program. This was the highly controversial Air Force program for housing Minuteman intercontinental ballistic missiles (ICBMs) according to a "shell-game" basing system. In the main scenario, a missile and several decoys would be moved randomly among ten or twenty possible buildings, so that the building with the real missiles could not be identified. All possible signatures, such as infrared signals or ground vibration, would be masked or be too small for detection. In principle, neither those nearby nor sensors in airplanes or satellites could tell which building held the real missile.

It was well known that the Air Force chief of staff at this time was a staunch MX promoter. Should it be a surprise that he reacted so violently to even the possibility of remote viewing?

Suppose the Soviets had developed a team of remote viewers? Could they detect, even at 10,000 miles, which building had the real missile? Even if results were not 100 percent, would not increasing the probability from one in ten to two or three in ten, or from one in twenty to three or four in twenty, still be better odds than any conventional detector could provide?

A proposal had been circulating in the Pentagon to explore just that possibility, and the former staffer was sure that the chief of staff had seen it. How better to squelch any potential threat to MX program approval than to deny that any potential threat existed, even from remote viewing? I have come to accept the former staffer's opinion: My DCI study program was withdrawn for political reasons only.

Not only was my DCI study program canceled, so was the remote viewing research activity with SRI. The shock wave of this irrational response also affected my personal activities. I was politely asked to discontinue my *Psychic Realm* course, to preclude any connection of the Air Force with psi phenomena.

So . . . the crash was extensive, exactly as that dream had foretold.

There was an aspect of the crash dream that was not clear. Why was I flying under a bridge? Why was I not higher off the ground, or at a higher level? That soon became clear.

Several weeks after the DCI program cancellation, I received an offer to join the Defense Intelligence Agency (DIA) in Washington, DC. I would be able to continue remote viewing research with SRI and coordinate application activities with an emerging Army remote viewing unit at Ft. Meade, Maryland. In a few months, I was in Washington, DC, pressing on with a variety of remote viewing activities. I was now flying above the bridge.

Immediately after my DCI program and remote viewing research cancellation, while still at FTD, I found myself in an incredibly ironic situation. Due to my connection with technology assessment and advanced sensor work, I was assigned to a special Air Force project. I was now a member of the MX Red Team, a group especially set up to do their best, using anticipated Soviet sensor capabilities, to counter the Air Force MX program! I knew better than to suggest that we look at Soviet remote viewing potential. As I sat through those meetings and walked around mock-up sites in the Nevada desert, I could only wonder what would happen if our Red Team actually uncovered a unique way for the Soviets to know which "shell" the MX was in.

Eventually, Congress canceled the MX shell-basing program. Logistically, it would have been a nightmare. It certainly had nightmare potential, as I already discovered the night of the *Airplane Crash* dream.

φ φ φ

Sometimes airplanes crash and flash brightly in psi's domain to guide us to their locations. Sometimes programs crash and we are forewarned in dreams of the night.

chapter four

Search for General D.

φ

During the days before moving to Washington, DC, I often walked around the neighborhood in Beavercreek, Ohio, pondering the unknown future. I visited my favorite stream in the forest adjacent to the Beavercreek High School. Tossing pebbles into one of the reflecting pools, I gazed intently at the ripples . . . wondering about similar ripples flowing from deep regions of the mind and psyche that reach out and interact with others.

I renewed my visions for locating missing airplanes and people. Global politics indicated that situations like the Iran hostages would occur in the future; I wanted to be prepared when we were thrust into another high-profile search project.

One of my responsibilities at the Defense Intelligence Agency (DIA) was coordinating remote viewing research and the Army application efforts at Ft. Meade.[9] How could research help applications?

There were two views: (1) we could not expect reliable applications until we understood the phenomenon better through research, or (2) we would learn more by doing exploratory applications than by researching. I understood both views and became an advocate of doing both; it became obvious that research and applications needed to be combined. I felt it best to consider all of what we were doing as exploratory. That would preclude unfounded claims being made and would recognize the fact that we were breaking into new territory.

One of the main problems was how to evaluate the data. Statistical approaches used in research could not be readily applied to application tasks because of the diversity of needs and types of projects. Some projects had one objective: Where is the missing object? Others were complex: What is at the remote site, and what is its purpose?

To help in understanding statistics better, as applied to psi research, I visited the parapsychology laboratory established by Dr. J. B. Rhine in Durham, North Carolina—now the Rhine Research Center. Dr. Louisa Rhine explained some of the difficulties in their early research and in having their work accepted by the scientific community, even though the statistics were valid and clearly showed nonchance results.

Returning with new enthusiasm, I pressed on in both research and applications. I renewed my own personal investigations but did not want to become directly involved in the program as a remote viewing data producer. I was comfortable with my role at that time as liaison, providing a bridge between management and the research/applications work. By December 1981, I was ready to plunge into operational remote viewing projects. I did not have to wait long.

We were contacted by representatives of the Secret Service who were interested in the location of an international terrorist, Carlos the Jackal. There was some suspicion that he had entered the United States and might do something to disrupt the annual Christmas tree-lighting ceremony held in the mall near the Capitol. Some people suspected that President Carter was in danger.

Remote viewers from SRI and the Ft. Meade unit worked on the task. No one perceived any dire perceptions concerning the tree-lighting ceremony. The consensus was that Carlos was somewhere in Africa—which was later verified. Gary Langford from SRI had a disturbing impression not related to the Christmas tree-lighting event. He perceived that an abduction event was about to occur involving a high-level political or military personage, but he did not think that this event related to President Carter or to anyone in Washington, DC. Since he was not sure where this event might happen, all we could do was record it and wait.

I entered Gary's data into my file on the evening of December 17, 1981 and left the office. The ceremony would be the next evening. Were we correct in saying the event would go as intended? What had Gary perceived, and to whom could it apply?

Around noon the next day I was called into the division chief's office. The news had just broken. Gary had been on track. Our organization and many others were about to become involved in a massive search activity. I read the news release over and over.

A high-ranking army officer, Brigadier General James Dozier,
stationed in Vorona, Italy, has been abducted by a terrorist group
known as the Red Brigades. U.S. and Italian authorities are
beginning an extensive search effort.

Here was another opportunity to use remote viewing in a search mission. I prepared procedures for integrating the data from the SRI research team and from the Ft. Meade unit. If any of the data showed consistency, we would provide it to the search team for addition to their other data sources. At this stage of our experience, we knew that psi data could have varying degrees of accuracy and could easily be misinterpreted, but I also knew from our own work and from reviewing police cases that psi sources could provide information that would be useful if interpreted and used properly. General sketches of areas where a missing person could be found, or impressions about some specific aspect of the criminal action, were often correct. Specific data, such as exact street addresses, would not be reasonable expectations from psi data, but I was sure that psi sources could narrow down the search possibilities and provide insight into General Dozier's state of health. Our involvement had to be kept unofficial and in perspective, away from the sensationalistic media. We had learned a lesson from the search project for that Soviet airplane.

In a few days, I had several written reports from select psi sensitives, but the data were diverse; which report was on track and which one was not? They might help narrow possibilities to general regions, such as "a town," or "rural area," but what town? What street? There was another problem: What if the General was being moved frequently? Analysts thought it likely that General Dozier was not being moved. If he were moved frequently, there would be too many risks for detection, especially with everyone on the lookout in Italy and throughout Europe.

I soon learned that psi sensitives from around the globe— most of them with little or no track record—were sending their impressions to various government agencies. In a few cases, unfortunately, this data went directly to contacts in the field without careful review or assessment. People unfamiliar with psi data usually interpret it literally. While speed of action in a crisis is critical, this is not always the best strategy for using psi data. If such reports were checked out and proven wrong, it would be highly unlikely that anyone would want to try a second time with other, and perhaps better, psi data.

There are several issues to consider when evaluating psi data. Are the initial impressions best, or are later data better? What about the source of the psi data? Are they from General Dozier's mind or from a consciousness field or consciousness hologram? What if General Dozier did not know where he was located or believed himself to be somewhere other than his true location? Would that make a difference? The only way to resolve such issues is to do search projects under a variety of conditions. Unfortunately, very few people had systematically studied the search and rescue potential of psi data. Some of the unsolicited psi data were checked out in the field and proven to be wrong. The media became aware of them and ridiculed the use of psi, which limited the chances for our remote viewing data to be considered by the search team. Nevertheless, we continued with our search activity, hoping that our remote viewers would be able to describe a specific location. We knew there was not much time—maybe only a few weeks. Previous Red Brigades abductees had not been released alive.

I renewed my personal investigations into psi and began to focus on "Where is General Dozier?" I was open to both remote viewing and psi dreams.

Initially, the impressions I received were related to current news stories or to current work situations. Nothing looked relevant. One evening, I decided to try for a precognitive dream of what I would read about General Dozier's status in a future newspaper. That night, I had a very disturbing dream: . . . *A military officer is murdered in a prison. Then I see he is alive and well, as if nothing had happened.*

The next evening the newspapers carried a disturbing story: *"General Dozier's death is set," caller says. A caller told the Italian newspapers today that General Dozier's body would be found that evening. "The body of the American will be placed in a village in the countryside, and police will soon find it," he said.* Perhaps my dream was on track after all. Why the sudden turnaround at its ending? Could this indicate that the death threat would not be carried out?

At noon the next day there was a news flash: *"Earlier news release on General Dozier's murder was a hoax . . ."* My dream was correct. During the following nights, I had other precognitive dreams on various technical and political issues. Their key elements also correlated to items in the newspapers the following day. I could see that a strategy change was needed. I had to get out of the near-term precognitive mode. Perhaps I needed a direct psi link-up with General Dozier, such as I experienced with Harold Sherman during the Coppermine River tracking experiment. I suspected that such rapport facilitated access to the "knowing," the "meaning" part of psi material and would help improve psi data accuracy.

One weekend afternoon in early January 1982, I took a long walk around Arlington Cemetery. I relaxed and let my thoughts and feelings flow. A great sense of peace, of history, of continuity, swept over me. I tried to reach out to General Dozier, wherever he was. I focused on General Dozier. I carried on an imaginary dialogue: "General, I would like to see if psi has potential to help find people like you who are held prisoner. Where are you? Where?" I walked over the Key Bridge and gazed into the dark Potomac River. I imagined whirlpools and tossing my request into them: "Find General Dozier."

That night, I had two brief dreams that were more like "image flashes." In one: *I see a sketch of a city with dark areas marked in its center and to the left.* In the other: *I am looking at a topographic map. There are tall mountains to the north. A circle is marked at an area toward the lower right side.* This scene was so brief I could hardly recall it. Even though I did not see many distinguishing features, I had the impression that I should pay attention to the east of the search area in Italy but not as far as the coast. Though this was not overly useful, I was encouraged. Perhaps more would follow. I sketched the scenes in my journal.

The following week was off to a fast start; I had a report due and a load of routine administrative matters to accomplish. I had little time to focus on the search for General D. He had now been missing for three weeks. I could sense despair creeping over the search effort. Neither Italian nor American search teams seemed to be making progress.

On Wednesday, January 13, 1982, a major snowstorm hit the East Coast that continued throughout the day and night. By early Thursday morning, the news media carried announcements that most government facilities were closed for the entire day. That meant a day off. I got up at my usual time anyway, walked to the 7-11 for coffee, and returned to my apartment with the intention of catching up on writing and routine chores. Later, I planned to hike around to take photographs and to simply enjoy the invigorating winter environment.

Around 9:00 A.M., I had an irresistible urge to go to the office. This was not a logical thing to do. No one would be there except security guards. The people I needed to interface with would not be available. I rationalized that it would be quiet and that I could get ahead on some work projects. I trudged through the snow, entered the deserted building, and began to review technical reports. I was the only one in the office.

About an hour later, the telephone broke the silence, ringing at the division chief's office. I took the message; it was from one of the few organizations active that day, and I learned the nature of the activity— it was the search for General Dozier! The technical data on advanced sensors that I had knowledge of was potentially useful in the search team's efforts in Italy. I attended an all-day meeting. At one point, the discussion drifted to psi phenomena, and I explained my role in the STARGATE project. This piqued their interest, as they had already been considering psi as a possible source of information for assisting in locating General Dozier. As I was about to leave, the official in charge asked, "How would you like to accompany Danny, our representative, to Italy? You might be able to see if remote viewing can be of any help."

I agreed to take the assignment, assuming that my own organization would approve. He wanted us to depart as soon as possible. This trip would give me a great opportunity to take a hard look at all the psi inputs I had received. There might be new information in the field that no one knew how to evaluate. We were scheduled to leave on January 18, 1982.

That night I had trouble falling asleep. The day's excitement, the anticipation of travel to Italy and direct involvement in the search for General Dozier weighed heavily on my mind. Shortly after I fell asleep, I "woke up" into a lucid dream, clearly aware that I was dreaming:

> *I am looking into a small room that has vivid blue walls. I try to get out by pushing against its side, and I feel it flex; it is made of soft fabric. Someone approaches. It is a woman with long, dark hair, deep eyes and prominent nose features. Our faces almost touch.*

Early the same morning, I had another vivid dream:

> *I am at a bus stop at a corner of a city block. I see the bus number, like 741 or 714. I think of traveling on this bus to the outskirts of a town or city. I lose something, like a wallet or jacket, and begin to look around. I walk into a small store that has books and magazines, tobacco, candy, ornamental objects, vegetables and many other items. I see the storeowner. He is of small stature and has Asian features. I ask him if he knows where my jacket is. He does; it is in the next room.*

If these dreams related to General Dozier's location, then the last one suggested a city/urban area, near or behind a general store. The small, soft-walled room of the first dream was hard to place—maybe the general was in a very confined space somewhere.

The next evening, I again had difficulty sleeping. Finally, around 3:00 A.M., I thought sleep had come. I couldn't be sure. I was aware of continuous thinking, without any visual imagery, while in a sleep-like state. Around 5:00 A.M., this "thinking-in" state broke into a vivid dream experience:

> *I am in an area that is cluttered with debris. There are at least four or five tough-looking people present. They are angry and are prone*

to fighting. An argument has occurred; broken green glass is scattered on the floor. I am aware that this place is near a large modern building or complex and an old institute or school. Then I am in a small room. The wall has two layers; the inner layer is soft, like paper, and can be easily pushed or penetrated.

Suddenly, a shift: I am in a public building looking at a display device. I see a picture of cosmonauts walking on the moon. They are oddly dressed and have large round heads. Their faces become animated and take on a mask-like appearance. They begin to look like apes. I notice equipment in the foreground. I realize I have seen this scene before and lose interest in it.

I return to the small room and notice a young couple. The woman has deep-set eyes with little luster. Her face has slight wrinkles and a few pockmarks or pimples. The man is not too tall but is broad shouldered and very strong. His face is stern; his eyes are partially closed. He has a hypnotic-like influence over the woman. She wants to break free and talk but can't. The people in this room leave and go to a nearby institute that is a training place for young people. The woman has injured her foot. I look at the soft wall and notice that the fabric has been torn.

I woke up with intense electrical or magnetic-like sensations. Cold waves swept over me, but certain areas of my head were very hot. A sense of energy pulsed through me. I could not sleep anymore and felt especially energized throughout the following day.

This may not have been a dream but an intense stream of images that occurred almost simultaneously when I was emerging from the hypnopompic prewaking state. I suspected that the moon landscape portion correlated to a remote viewing picture target I had set up weeks ago. The sudden search crisis had distracted me from completing that project. If this was in fact a "psi intrusion," then the other parts of the dream were likely psi experiences and could relate to my primary concern: Where is General Dozier? With great anticipation, I checked the sealed target package: There was my moon landscape! The target page in the magazine showed a computer game arcade. A large room was filled with panels and displays. Paintings of a moonlike landscape, filled with strange insects, covered the large panels in the foreground. They had large heads and resembled astronauts in space suits. Several months earlier, a similar picture came up as the target. Now I could see why the scene felt familiar and why I had lost interest in it.

This correlation gave me confidence that the remainder of the dream had a connection with General D. The dream imagery indicated a location in a modern building near a large school. The people in the dream were not compatible, and one of them wanted to break free. I associated the broken green glass with drugs due to its symbolic connection with drugs that I had noted in disturbing dreams of a few *Psychic Realm* class members.

The night before we were to leave for Italy, I had another vivid dream:

> *I see a large city with a wide river winding through its center. Then I am in a tent. A woman is handing something to me, like a metal pot of tea or coffee. A small drawer is nearby with odd items in it. I leave the tent, crawling between small ropes. The tent is very small and made of canvas. I see people in jogging or ski-type clothes. I have a flashlight and swing it around the area, like a small beacon. I shine it into the eyes of one of the men. He is surprised. I tell him I only want to help; he becomes curious about the flashlight and wants to know how it flashes. I give it to him and he blinks it on and off several times. Outside, I notice a large, wide street.*

The flashlight could represent emotions or needs flashing in psi space. The tent imagery was puzzling and could be symbolic of tight confinement. Maybe the idea of "telepathic communication" had become acceptable to General D. Was he, either through a feeling of desperation, or prompted by deeper experiences from within himself, considering psi communication? Long periods of confinement, and presumably long sleep periods, might in fact be opening up his own psi awareness.

As I considered this interpretation, I felt it was reasonable. In a similar situation, the first thing I would do would be to "reach out mentally" to someone like Harold Sherman or others with whom I have had good psi communication success. I am quite confident they could immediately perceive highly accurate data about me and my location. Whom might General Dozier be trying to reach? Since he had no knowledge of STARGATE, might he be trying to reach out mentally to his wife? I wondered if she had any familiarity with psi. Perhaps the spouses of those held captive should immediately be given a crash course in psi, meditation and dreams. They might be the best psi teammates available.

Was I reading too much into the blinking flashlight dream incident? Perhaps I was. But the dream did evoke a new sense of confidence. Would my psi impressions improve?

The next day, Danny and I left for Europe. We had to route through the European Command in Stuttgart, Germany, to coordinate our trip to Italy with the European Command Headquarters. Then we traveled to Vicenza and Camp Eberle, the U.S. search team's base of operation. Danny and I were quickly thrown into the action of our official tasks. I asked to review the psi data they had received from unsolicited sources, although I was informed that no psychic data was being considered at this time.

The impressions were all over the map. Why did so many people send them in? Were they sincerely trying to help, or were they on some sort of ego trip? Take a shot; it just might work, they may have thought. Maybe I was too tired at this point. I certainly was disgusted. Very few of those several hundred letters gave any insight into the sender's credentials or past experiences in search projects. Some claimed they had helped their local police in solving crimes, but there were no specifics. I could now easily see why the search authorities were currently disregarding anything from psychic sources.

What a dilemma. After reviewing those letters, I gained empathy for the search team. From my own experiences, I knew that psi could be helpful in search projects, but to be reliable, a dedicated effort with proven talent was required.

The next day was Saturday, January 23, 1982. General Dozier had been missing for over five weeks. Hope for his rescue was slipping away, and search activity was slowing down. I took another look at the psychic inputs I had previously reviewed. Nothing compelling struck me, even after a good night's rest.

That evening, I walked the streets of Vicenza for several hours, focusing on the goal: "Where is General Dozier?" Before sleep, I visualized the general: "OK, General, I am now much closer to you. Where are you? Where?" I drifted into a deep sleep. Early in the morning I woke from a brief dream:

> *I see a large building. Then I am looking into a small room. I see a dark-haired woman with prominent nose features and a man who reminds me of someone I worked with years ago. Then I am in a marketplace, looking at vegetables and fruit. A clerk, who looks like the man I saw earlier, is holding two large bags of groceries. A tall military man tells me that I will soon get into that small room. Then I am outside, returning to the large building. It is on a wide street on an uphill slope.*

This dream had a clear association to a grocery store or a marketplace. The woman was the same one I had seen in earlier dreams. The men were new dream images. The one who appeared twice in different roles reminded me of a work acquaintance. I felt that the emphasis on him was important. Perhaps he closely resembled one of the terrorists, or maybe his name might have a relevant association. Sometimes in psi dreams a name has significance and even for hidden targets the first few letters of a name are often correct. As I thought of the dream image, I felt that his last name, "DeRoze," was more significant than his first name. If so, perhaps a name like De, or Der, or possibly Ro, might be relevant. The tall military figure at the end seemed out of place. What did his cryptic words *You will soon get into that room* mean? The ending of the dream called attention to a large building. Maybe I was sensing General Dozier's location.

It was now Sunday, January 24, 1982. Each day gave us new insight into the difficulties of searching for a hostage, especially in a foreign country. I reviewed new letters sent to the field but they had nothing useful. I had not received any updates from the remote viewers at Ft. Meade or SRI. Late that night, I woke from an intense dream:

I am looking at a grocery store at the corner of a city block. I move inside to a narrow stairwell with light green walls and go up to the second floor. A dark-haired woman with prominent nose features walks past. I see her go to the street to meet an elderly couple who have arrived in a large black limousine. I look inside the car and see a coffin.

The elderly couple seemed to be out of place, but the dark-haired woman was the same one who had appeared in other recent dreams. If this dream was on track, it indicated that General Dozier was being held in a second-story apartment above a grocery store. It conveyed a clear sense of urgency; General Dozier's ordeal was about to end tragically. The coffin clearly symbolized death.

On Tuesday, January 26, Danny and I had to travel to Verona to coordinate a few technical issues. I tried to focus on "Where is General Dozier?," hoping to pick up an intuitive feeling that might signal his presence should he actually be somewhere in Verona. Nothing. Verona felt "cold." This was not the place.

The search team was becoming increasingly concerned. They were sure General Dozier's situation was about to become tragic. If he had any chance of survival, someone had to find him soon. The tension grew more intense. I, too, was becoming convinced that time was running out. The "coffin" image of that recent dream was highly disturbing. I took another look at all the data I had received from the remote viewers at Ft. Meade but could not narrow search possibilities to any specific area. As I studied a detailed topographic map of North Italy, I noticed that some features correlated to the imagery and dreams I had experienced, the best fit being between Vicenza and Venice—at Padua. If Padua, then where in Padua? I had no choice at this time but to consider my own impressions. They were reasonably specific, and I had confidence in them. They felt right, and they had symbolic connections to General Dozier. My first choice was a small second-floor apartment in a large building above a corner grocery store. An early dream called attention to the center or the southwest section of a city. One dream had a large school or institute nearby.

Late that day, I met with one of the search officials. He was not at all open to psi, yet I felt that I had to inform him of my deductions. I showed him the relief map, along with the select sketches I had made, and said, "My best deduction is that General Dozier is somewhere in Padua." I handed him a page summarizing my impressions.

"Thanks, but no thanks." he said tersely. "I can tell you that is not the place. Milan, Venice, some other city, but not Padua. We are beginning to suspect he is not even in a large city."

What could I say? I had done what I could. There was no point in going any further. Then he was interrupted, and our meeting was cut short. I returned to my desk, certain that he was wrong. That evening, I walked the streets of Vicenza for a long time. A thick fog settled over the city; a sense of timelessness swept through me. It seemed as if I had been in northern Italy forever. When was the search for General Dozier going to end? I wondered how the general felt. As I walked on through the fog, a deep sense of connection grew stronger—at times, I felt as if I were in his place. I could feel his sense of hope and despair. Someone had to find him . . . soon.

Next morning, Danny and I caught a taxi to the airport at Venice, en route to a meeting at the embassy in Rome. About halfway to Venice, a large sign appeared out of the fog—Padua! The instant I saw it, something more than glaring light hit me. Without thought, I blurted out, "This is it! This is the place! I am sure of it!" It was an unconscious reflex as in a word association test. Then we were past the exit. "Padua," I said, "is the city where General Dozier is being held. I'm sure of it now." We sped on through the morning fog and mist. Soon we were at the airport, then Rome. Perhaps we could find a way to drive through Padua on our return. Maybe something might seem familiar.

General Dozier had been missing for six weeks. It was easy to sense that tension at the embassy was climbing to new heights. I remained convinced that he was in Padua.

The next morning, January 28, 1982, I was in a restaurant updating my journal. A woman came to my table and started to talk. "Hello," she said in a friendly tone. "You Americans must be very happy today."

"Happy? Why?" I asked, puzzled.

"You mean you haven't heard? Your General Dozier was rescued today by the Italians. He is free and well." I stared at her. She continued, "Yes, his rescue is on all the news programs."

"You mean the search is over!" I exclaimed. "Oh, how incredible!"

"Yes," she said. "He was held in an apartment in Padua."

I could hardly believe this news. Quickly, I returned to the embassy, which was in chaos. No point staying on—our meetings were no longer necessary. I met Danny and we rescheduled a flight back to Vicenza. General Dozier would be there by the time we returned.

The weather that evening was clear. As we flew north, a wall of gold-tinted Alpine peaks rose from the horizon. To the west, the lights of Padua broke through the darkening shadows. A silver path curved from the foothills, then turned east, through Padua. It was the Brenta River, moving slowly toward the dark Adriatic Sea. Somewhere below in Padua was that secret place. Now the whole world knew where it was.

Vicenza had undergone a transformation. It seemed that several armies had invaded. Military trucks, tanks and heavy-duty weapon carriers jammed the streets. Troops heavily laden with pistols, rifles and submachine guns crowded the sidewalks. Guards were packed tightly around Camp Eberle. Sentries were on rooftops. It seemed like a war zone. Simply getting on base, even with a proper pass, was difficult.

I gathered all the information I could regarding General Dozier's dramatic rescue. In brief: Italian authorities had five days earlier located a Red Brigades member who provided clues that led to General Dozier's location. Italian commandos, the Leatherheads unit, then stormed into that apartment in Padua. In ninety seconds the raid was over, and General Dozier had been rescued.

The apartment was on the second floor of an eight-story building, directly above Dea's Supermarket. It was on Piedemonte Street, in the southwest section of the city, near the University of Padua. The apartment was rented to the daughter of a well-known Paduan surgeon.

When the commandos stormed the door, they overpowered one of the terrorists, who was carrying two bags of groceries. Another terrorist was pointing a gun at General Dozier but had no time to react. There were four terrorists in the room, three men and one woman. The woman was the leader's companion.

General Dozier had been confined inside a small tent in the middle room of a three-room apartment above the front of the store. He was clothed in a jogging outfit, as were the terrorists.

As I received this information, I could see that my images and dreams correlated well with General Dozier's situation. The latest dreams were specific; one of my sketches resembled the building. The small tent that appeared in at least three of my dreams now made sense. The woman in the dream resembled the terrorist. The association to drugs was very apt; drugs had played a role in how the police obtained information on who knew General Dozier's location.

Later, I learned that General Dozier had passed the time with games that he improvised. He kept in shape by practicing yoga exercises for long periods. Initially, he did not know his location. He was sure it was a large city, but he did not know which one until a few weeks after his abduction. At that time, he became open to the possibility of telepathy. He began to concentrate on his wife, Judith, hoping she could pick up something about his location, his condition and his feelings. He had lost hope that he would be found by ordinary means. Occasionally, he would hear one of the terrorists "hammering something." He thought they were constructing a box to move him to a new location—or maybe they were building a coffin. His focus on psi communication increased as the weeks went on and as the carpentry continued.

When I reviewed my journal, I wondered if the dream five days before his release, when a *tall military man tells me that I will soon get into that room* symbolized the beginning of events leading to General Dozier's rescue.

The dream of January 16, eleven days before his rescue, had the blinking flashlight. This imagery corresponded to the time when General Dozier began his attempts to communicate telepathically with Judith.

As I reviewed my journal from December 17, 1981 to the time of the general's release six weeks later, it became apparent that my dreams had painted consistent pictures. Their accuracy began to improve when I arrived in Italy, probably from my increased motivation or from

General Dozier's mental focus. I do not think the shorter distance was responsible. I suspected that his thoughts were like beacons, mentally swinging and flashing intense signals into the night, crying out, "Does anyone hear me? I am in . . . Padua."

Later I learned that one of the remote viewers at Ft. Meade had sent his recent impressions to my office in Washington, DC. That information was on my desk and had not been sent to the field. The note stated: . . . *A strong impression popped into my mind today. I believe General Dozier is in Padua.* It had a sketch of a city area with the word "Padua" written on it. This impression was received around the time General Dozier became aware of his location and began his focusing on telepathic contact.

The search team packed to leave Italy. I was thankful for the opportunity to be with them and to explore the potential of psi phenomena for a critical search mission. I could see that under proper circumstances, with dedicated and motivated people, psi could play an important role in difficult missions. I closed my journal and walked around Camp Eberle, wondering about . . . dreaming of . . . searches to come.

In the decades and centuries ahead, using psi in search and rescue projects will be easier. I did not want to dream that far ahead. Something should be possible now, even at our current level of evolution. Difficult, yes, but possible. I intended to keep trying. When I had first arrived in Vicenza, the hard-nosed search official said something that I found inspirational: "He who searches, finds." I agree. We were both searching in different styles; maybe someday we can be open partners.

chapter five

On the Run

φ

One evening shortly after my return from Italy and the search for General Dozier, I retreated to my favorite window seat in the Top of the Town restaurant in the Prospect House to review our search activity. Someone had scratched a small portion of the tinted covering from the window to expose clear glass. It gave the impression of "looking through a glass darkly." The vista toward Washington, DC was occluded except for that hole-like effect. As I gazed at that small opening it seemed as if I was peeking through a barrier into another dimension.

In a similar way, I and the others searching for General Dozier had caught a glimpse of another region, another dimension—one that is an exact counterpart of the three-dimensional world that we call real. That other dimension, space or region is accessible with the proper shift of mind-focus—something like turning the dial, or frequency shifting, a radio or television. Our remote viewing impressions may not be truly remote. Maybe what we access is shifting attention to another corner of our psyche to a far-reaching theater of our mind. It does not matter how we achieve this shift of focus—awake and relaxed or asleep and dreaming. Our inner stage director makes all the arrangements and the appropriate connections and opens the curtain.

I wrote a summary of our search saga, knowing that the role of STARGATE in the search for General Dozier could not become public knowledge for years or decades. I was reluctant to add my own experiences, since they were not an official part of the effort. I felt they were meaningful, so I did include them but disguised their source and the mode. Considerable misunderstanding existed in the general public, and even among some STARGATE personnel, about the dream state. I consider the dream state to be the easiest mode for experiencing psi impressions, including descriptions of distant places, the original emphasis of remote viewing. Our theater of the mind does not care how we label or elicit psi perceptions.

At this point in our remote viewing activity we had been working with fixed targets. The objective of the remote viewing project was to describe an area fixed in space and time; the target did not move around from day to day. What if General Dozier had been moved? Even if remote viewers were able to keep up with the new locations, what good would that do? The data would be history by the time any feasible action could be taken. To be useful in this situation, our psi data had to be predictive or precognitive, and it had to be synchronized with the search team's ability to intersect with the future path of the hostage.

Moving target searches seemed impractical, even impossible. But STARGATE provided evidence that a future target could be perceived. Several projects at SRI provided statistical evidence that remote viewers could describe a picture or a place that had not yet been identified by anyone. In a typical experiment involving this type of precognition, a remote viewer's task is to describe the picture that will be randomly selected tomorrow at 2:00 P.M. The remote viewer provides a sketch of what that future target will look like. The next day, the target is actually chosen at 2:00 P.M. Some remote viewers were able to provide near-picture-perfect sketches of that target coming toward them from the future.

Since precognition of this type can be demonstrated in the laboratory when no one knows what the target will be, then precognition can be called upon for locating missing people, such as hostages or fugitives, who are moving. As I mused over this type of search, it became clear that the path of those searching also had to be part of the dynamics. It was no good to be a day behind or ahead of a fugitive on the run. Two paths—the fugitive and the searchers—had to intersect. Sometimes the intersection window could be broad, perhaps several hours or days; other times it could only be minutes. I surmised that locating people in transit should be easier than describing a picture to be selected by a random computer event, since people's intentions can be perceived.

There were some conceptual difficulties. A few of those involved in the early remote viewing work felt that remote viewing would not be effective for moving targets. As I reviewed the data, it appeared to me that they were definition-locking themselves. They did not believe it would work; therefore, it would not—at least for them. Some of the concepts or interpretations of remote viewing had to be expanded in order to fit the experimental evidence. The best approach, it seemed to me, was to simply take on a moving target search and phrase the objective correctly. For example, the remote viewing task would be defined as "Locate where and by when the hostage can be found." Having established a framework and overall philosophy, I felt that I would be prepared should a moving target search project come our way.

Some of the results of psi sensitives involved in police or detective work were impressive. One psi sensitive in Maine, Shirley Harrison, accurately tracked the location of a child abducted from his home. As later information verified, she was able to describe the correct city and street names where the child was held. She also sketched a building that matched the actual location.

It took several days to check out the information, and by that time the abductor had moved. Shirley then attempted to describe where he was headed and was able to name a specific city and a motel. The client called directory assistance and discovered that such a motel existed. She asked to be connected with the person who was known to be moving the child around. That person was in fact registered there. He left immediately when the call came through, suspecting that the police had located him.[10]

Examples like this from credible psi sensitives led me to accept that psi phenomena—remote viewing or any other name we wanted to give it—had potential for locating a moving target.

Synchronicities, also known as meaningful coincidences, provide strong evidence for the role of psi in bringing about an appropriate intersection of paths. Synchronicities are common experiences that happen to almost everyone. We are in the right place at the right time and receive unexpected help. I saw little difference between synchronistic experiences and a remote viewing project in which we were actively looking for a moving target.

In synchronicities we are usually unaware of the approaching incident, but our subconscious mind knows what is about to happen. We are drawn to the right place through hunches, urges and intuitions. In remote viewing, the unconscious knowledge of where that target will be becomes conscious. Sketches can be made; the area might even be named. Not all possible future paths may be able to intersect. The area may be inaccessible, the pace of the traveler too fast.

I was prepared for a moving target search project, and eventually one came my way.

In February 1988, I was called into a meeting with the division chief; from his expression I knew we were about to be thrown into another search.

"Have you heard the news? A Marine, Lieutenant Colonel William Higgins, has been abducted in Lebanon. Are you ready for another search mission?"

"I am always ready. We'll take a look," I said calmly.

Thus, STARGATE began another challenging search for a missing person. We were fully aware of the difficulty of searching in a foreign country, especially when terrorist groups are involved that can readily move about.

I mobilized the STARGATE team, and we went full speed into the search for Lt. Col. Higgins. The first few days were fast-paced. Our remote viewing data had a role in directing where other sensors should focus. We received almost immediate feedback and were able to develop a route that the abductors were taking. Remote viewing information identified the vehicle types and people involved. One remote viewer's sketches matched a specific area, including a uniquely shaped building that was identified on aerial photographs.

Weeks later, another captive was released who verified that Lt. Col. Higgins was actually in that building at the time the sketch was made. We were elated. We knew that he was being moved frequently and tried to keep ahead of the terrorists' route. After a few weeks we felt that something unfortunate had happened. One of the remote viewers who had previously demonstrated a good track record in describing people, perceived deep water that invoked a cold, uneasy feeling. Impressions from other remote viewers diverged widely. We were unable to keep tracking Lt. Col. Higgins's location. Months later, we learned that Lt. Col. Higgins had been murdered around the time of these uneasy feelings.

This unfortunate incident did provide a chance to test psi under field conditions when the target is moving. We were able to set up workable procedures and quickly respond to operational questions.

I wondered what would have happened if Lt. Col. Higgins had considered the reality of psi, as General Dozier had done. What if he had begun visualizing his environment and focused on connecting with expectant remote viewers? I felt certain that some information came through without his taking an active role, but I suspected that remote viewing data would have improved had he knows about STARGATE and focused on psi contact. Our involvement would have increased his morale and hope.

More search projects came our way. Through contacts with the U.S. Coast Guard and other agencies, we set up exploratory projects to use remote viewing in some of their drug search missions. This developed into a major effort for the STARGATE unit. Most Coast Guard officials welcomed our well-qualified and exploratory approach. Others were uncomfortable and reluctant to admit our involvement— and our successes.

A typical drug search project was "Here is a photograph of a ship. Is it carrying illegal drugs? If so, what type, where are they located on the ship, and where is the ship going?" These were tough questions but good ones. They are the same questions any drug enforcement official would ask. We learned that only a few of the suspect ships could be boarded even if found, due to limited manpower resources. Our task was to narrow down search possibilities so that boarding and searching would be successful.

We launched into this exciting search activity with great enthusiasm. Some of the early results, according to our contacts, were spectacular. In one instance, remote viewing data indicated the location of a ship in the North Pacific that had originated in Hong Kong. It could have been anywhere in the Pacific. Reconnaissance missions acted on our information and found it very close to our location on the day we had predicted. As a Coast Guard vessel caught up with it, the crew of the target ship tossed an estimated seven tons of drugs overboard and set fire to the ship. While being towed to Honolulu, it sank.

A ship last seen along the Florida coast was predicted by a remote viewer to be fifty miles off the New Jersey coast, east of Atlantic City. A reconnaissance plane acted on that information and sighted it in that vicinity.

In several instances, remote viewers sketched the exact locations where drugs were hidden on small vessels. The search of a small island led to a drug cache almost exactly where a remote viewer had indicated on a crudely drawn sketch of the island.

Remote viewers described the use of a tunnel used in smuggling drugs under the Mexican-U.S. border. This was later verified.

There were instances where the ship or the drug cache could not be found. A few of these misses involved rapidly developing events. In some of these cases there was evidence that the drugs had been recently moved from the indicated location. The crew may have been warned that a search of the ship was about to happen.

In some situations we were able to be on site in various ports during the search. Some of us felt this proximity enhanced the remote viewing accuracy; others felt that being close to the target did not matter. Logistics was always a problem; we certainly did not want the media to know of our activities. We knew how damaging media coverage can be for such an activity.

Our later efforts for drug enforcement tasks were difficult to evaluate. Less supportive contact people became involved, limiting our feedback. Logistical response time lagged; targets appeared to be moving about more rapidly, and our data were not acted upon in timely fashion for evaluation. The potential of STARGATE was not fully realized.

During the time when we were undertaking search missions for moving drug targets, another great search opportunity came our way—it was the type of search I had always envisioned. I listened intently as an assistant commissioner for the U.S. Customs Service said, "This guy is on the run—find him! We want his butt!"

I was looking at a photograph of a fugitive. This man, Charles (Charlie) Frank Jordan (C. J.),[11] had been a Customs agent stationed in South Florida. For many years, he had been an outstanding and trustworthy employee and had frequently led the charge to uncover drug-smuggling activity in the Florida Keys and along the south coast of Florida. But when drug interdiction missions began to fail, it became clear that the smugglers were being forewarned from the inside. The U.S. Customs Service and the Drug Enforcement Agency (DEA) discovered that Charlie was the informant. When he learned of their suspicion, he became a fugitive. An intensive search failed to locate him. Several years after his disappearance, he was featured on the *America's Most Wanted* television program. His extensive background in the Caribbean area and in Panama led authorities to suspect he had gone into hiding somewhere in that region.

Even after years had passed, Charlie Jordan's name still evoked the intense ire of the U.S. Customs Service and the DEA. There was no question about the importance of the search. Only the airplane search in Africa and the General Dozier case had invoked such strong feelings among those involved. The intensity of the Customs official's gaze at the photograph of Charlie Jordan, and then at me, removed any doubt. This official really did want Charlie's butt—and the rest of Charlie, too.

I assured him that we would give this our best effort but could not guarantee results. "Look," he said determinedly, "I don't care if you can only give me odds like 1 in 10, or something worse. I'll take it! Nothing else has worked. Even if 1 in 10, then for projects like this, that 1 would be a miracle. Shall I tell you how much our search for Charlie has cost us to date?"

I did not ask. Clearly, if we could hit the target on this project, even if that success was followed by ten failures, this man would be extremely happy. So would we. I left that meeting feeling highly motivated. If I could convey that feeling to the STARGATE remote viewers, then we had a better chance to crack this case wide open.

I met with my STARGATE staff and described the task. It was very simple: Do what you can to locate Charlie Jordan. I showed them his photograph and informed them that he was a fugitive who could be anywhere on earth. I had not wanted to know anything about him and had asked to be kept blind of any background information. Prior to that meeting, I had not even heard of C. J.—neither had any of the remote viewers.

Each viewer had his or her own cognitive style, but two basic approaches were used in our program. A few relied on spontaneous impressions, with little or no anticipated sequence. Others preferred to use a strategy that they felt helped them develop remote viewing impressions in an orderly manner. From what I observed in many tasks, it did not matter which strategy was followed. Ultimately, the data spoke for themselves.

Some remote viewers had a better track record when describing areas and configurations; others were better with personal aspects. For a search project, both configurations (i.e., landmarks) and personal types (i.e., the person's feelings and thoughts) come into play. My challenge was to correlate the data and decide what was relevant. This meant examining the impressions from all the viewers to look for patterns and consistencies. If their impressions differed widely, then I would have to make a judgment about which ones should receive more consideration than the others. I usually did this by considering the individuals' track records, their preferences and cognitive styles, and subjective factors such as how strongly they felt about their impressions. Strength of feeling was hard to judge, but I had developed a sense for it.

Whatever would happen, I was sure that they all felt the intensity of need I had conveyed. I had learned over the years that degree of need or importance makes the difference between good and incomplete results. One can be highly self-motivated, but it certainly helps to hear or feel urgency from those to whom you are providing a service.

Within the next few days, the four remote viewers assigned to this case worked on the task of finding C. J. Sketches from those who preferred a structural approach were generally of flat rural areas, possibly near a large city. The viewer who followed a spontaneous style had stated, "He is in Wyoming, near a place that sounds like Lowell. There is an Indian burial place nearby." That was quite specific, and if on track, definitely narrowed down the search possibilities. We then examined a map of Wyoming and located a town, Lovell, similar to the name she had perceived, near the Montana border. She was sure that he was somewhere in the northwest part of Wyoming, even if not exactly in Lovell.

Since the cognitive style of this remote viewer favored personal rapport, I suspected that she had accessed what Charlie Jordan knew: either where he was or where he intended to be in the near future. I decided to list her impressions as the most likely. I prepared a page summary of all our results and read them over the phone to the Customs Service contact assigned to work with us. He listened quietly.

"So your first choice is in northwest Wyoming. Well," he slowly responded, "I can tell you emphatically—no. None of those responses make any sense. We are certain he never left the Caribbean and is somewhere on one of the islands. Sorry."

He thanked me for our efforts. I sent a formal letter with our results to his office for the records. Unbeknownst to me, however, the chief of that office did send out a general alert—a BOLO (be on the lookout) to agents in the Northwest area of the United States, asking them to be on the lookout for Charlie Jordan.

Given the comments of my Customs Service contact, I did not see any point in continuing the search for C. J. None of the remote viewers had perceived him in a Caribbean or ocean area. We obviously had blown this extremely important task. I found it odd that we had done so poorly on a project with such extremely high need. That did not track with our prior experiences.

Several weeks passed. I could not get the search for C. J. out of my mind. It was too important to ignore. Maybe we should try again, although by then we all had seen a copy of the *America's Most Wanted* program that had featured Charlie Jordan. Even if he was in the Caribbean, then where? The task of finding C. J. still remained. I could still hear the Customs official's stern voice: "We want his butt!"

Then one night, after brooding over "finding C. J.," I had a very unusual dream.

> *I am walking around in a large resort area and see people playing games. Tall snow-capped mountains are in the distance. I walk into a lodge and wait in line to buy film for my camera. Someone walks by who is ill-kempt and unshaven.*

I woke up, surprised. The mountain scene was vivid and resembled the Rockies. The ill-kempt man seemed out of place in the lodge. I fell asleep and soon woke from another dream:

> *I am at a mountain resort area in a campground. There are trailers and tents all around me. Ahead, I see a small play area with people throwing something like a Frisbee. I walk along a path to a fast-flowing river. Several large yellow boulders are visible. The water in the river is silt-colored. I walk along the shore and notice that it is covered with small yellow stones. Then I return to the campground. The air feels cool.*

I woke up, startled at the vividness of this dream. It was like being in a real mountain setting. I was puzzled by the murky river and the yellow boulders and stones. In all the mountains I had traveled in, the rivers and streams were crystal clear, not silt-colored. The dominance of yellow silted water, yellow boulders, yellow stones was puzzling.

Later that evening I took another look at those dreams. Maybe they related to Charlie Jordan. If they did, then they were clearly consistent with the northwest Wyoming location identified by the one remote viewer. I planned to ask the STARGATE remote viewers to do another search for C. J. the next day, but I was overtaken by events. Early the same day, the remote viewer who had perceived the northwest Wyoming location had an impression about C. J. during a remote viewing session on an unrelated issue. It was like a powerful intrusion that stirred up her emotions.

What she told me was very clear: "Tell your Customs contact that if they want Charlie Jordan, they'd better act fast! He is preparing to leave the area and travel west along the Montana-Wyoming border. He is still in that region . . . but not for long."

What brought about this sudden outburst ? Was she correct? Were the Customs agents wrong about the Caribbean?

Reluctantly, I called my Customs Service contact and told him of her latest impressions. But he would not budge. He reminded me that C. J. was in the Caribbean. At least, it was clear that their expectations were not interfering with our psi impressions!

It would be a shame if our data could lead to finding C. J. and was not used. How would we know? If C. J. was in Wyoming and about to move on, he could go anywhere. Unless he was eventually captured, no one would ever know where he had been at this time, and it would be impossible to know how close, or far off, our impressions had been.

That evening, I wrote a brief account of the C. J. search in my journal and took another look at those recent dreams. They were too vivid to ignore; I was sure they had relevance to the search. They were consistent with the remote viewer's impressions and fit the landscape of northwest Wyoming. There are certainly many lodges and campsites throughout that region, especially in and around Yellowstone National Park.

Early the next morning, I received a call from my Customs Service contact.

"I called to tell you something," he said, in an extremely apologetic tone of voice. "I want to inform you that yesterday an alert state trooper caught sight of Charlie Jordan entering a camping area near Yellowstone National Park. Our agents quickly came in and were able to apprehend him without a struggle. He was living in a trailer in that campground."

Great! Now I could relax and close this case. The notice sent out by the assistant commissioner of U.S. Customs Service had led to increased awareness by law enforcement people that eventually led to C. J.'s capture. The STARGATE remote viewer was on track, and her information had been acted upon.

For several years, Charlie Jordan had been moving from campground to campground across the country in an Airstream camper trailer. The campground where he was captured was near the south side of Yellowstone National Park. An Indian burial ground was nearby. His trailer was parked along a small, fast-flowing stream. Not far away was a large river, the Yellowstone.

That evening as I updated my journal, I could not help but chuckle when I reviewed that last dream . . . *campground . . . silt-colored, fast-flowing river . . . mountain resort area . . . yellow boulders . . . yellow stones.*

Of course: Yellowstone.

PART
2

River Shadows

ivers spread out in delta regions to merge with their source and begin another river cycle. They are forced together at confluences where diverse streams meet.

River currents generate turbulence that creates interference patterns. Sometimes their waves become larger; sometimes they shrink and disappear. The strength of these waves can be judged by examining the shadows they create. If we look far ahead out across the water, we can see these waves and shadows and predict if they are likely to arrive at our shore.

In this section, *Confluences* reviews issues and conflicts that psi phenomena can invoke. *Delta Regions* considers implications from psi research and quantum physics for the existence of a consciousness field. *Reflections* has thoughts on the significance of psi, co-creative principles, and *river dreams*.

111

Confluences

φ

River confluences are places where two or more rivers join to form a larger stream. They are usually of two types: smooth or chaotic. If the rivers coming together are similar, the confluence is not noticeable. The rivers combine with hardly a ripple, barely a murmur. Their combined water flows smoothly downstream. But if the connecting rivers are significantly different in size or flow rate, are full of boulders or have other differing features, then the confluence can be turbulent and even ferocious. In both situations, the water is the same substance. But one meeting is accepting and smooth; the other is filled with high wave barriers and rocky resistances. The different steams clash and crash together. For turbulent confluences, it may be a long time before the combined rivers mix uniformly and coherently.

Sometimes the turbulence when diverse rivers meet is not as frightening as it initially appears to be. The deafening sound of churning cascades may become less troubling as time passes and we become accustomed to the noise. When we move closer to the shoreline, we may discover gentle currents intermingled with the chaotic surges. Sometimes we can enter the roiling streams, learn how to move with their swirling currents, and travel across the troubled water unharmed.

River confluences are like dynamic mirrors. They let us see aspects of ourselves, reminding us of the ways in which we can interact with others. When we confluence with those who are similar to us, our meetings are accepting and smooth. When their beliefs, ideas, experience base are different from ours, our confluence is most likely to be filled with resistance and barriers. Very often, the main turbulence is in our stream, not in theirs.

Psi is a natural part of the universe and resembles a talent that anyone can uncover and develop in varying degrees. Reasons for resistance, even fear, of psi are cultural and psychological and are not inherent in the phenomena. It has a built-in censor or filter; those who open their psi gates are not swamped by psi if they maintain physical and psychological balance. No one is able to apply psi in a negative sense unless others have somehow consented. When we desire to establish a psi connection with individuals based on mutual trust, then we can interact with them in positive ways, no matter where they are located. We can know what they desire us to be aware of; we can assist in their physical and psychological well-being in a healing sense. Our psi connectivity functions best when the issue is important and mutually beneficial.

The psi process has a role in how some aspect of memory is retained and accessed. It provides the link between conscious intentions and the resulting brain activity. It has pathways for interacting with specialized domains of our collective unconscious, such as

mystical or transcendental regions, or possibly even with the consciousness of other intelligent sources in the universe.

Over the years, I have discovered that the topic of psi—parapsychology, psychic abilities, telepathy, clairvoyance, remote viewing—
creates turbulent reactions in many people. Barriers and resistances are
immediately apparent. Their confluence with even the idea of psi is a
deeply disturbing experience for them. Reasons, if any can be readily
identified, vary greatly, but they are of two general types: those that
deny the reality of psi and those that relate to interpretations of psi.

Clash of Realities

There are several specific reasons that psi is rejected or denied. The
main objections to the reality of psi is that there is no scientific theory
that explains it. Therefore, it cannot exist. The critics also claim that
after more than a century of psi research, the phenomena are still not
proven. Consequently, psi research is labeled as a "pseudoscience" and
rejected as a valid endeavor.

Even when psi experiments show positive results (i.e., exceed
chance expectation), critics give a variety of hypotheses as to why the
experiment seemed to succeed. These reasons include improper experimental controls, inadvertent clues or even fraud. Occasionally, hostile
critics will reject the results because they suspect that the researcher
has subjective reasons for wanting to believe in psi, and therefore
anything the researcher does is suspect.

Critics do not consider spontaneous psi incidents as valid, since in
their view the experiencer has misinterpreted a chance event, deduced
it from inferences or clues, or purposefully distorted the accounts.

No Scientific Theory

This is not—and never has been—a prerequisite for a phenomenon's
existence. Most scientific discoveries have preceded theory. Theory is

based on observation, measurement and deduction; it is developed by the study of "what happens." Sometimes the phenomena are very subtle and are considered anomalies or even ignored until found to reveal new truths. Newton's synthesis of planetary orbits and things that fall came from direct observation and experience. The discovery of the anomaly now called radioactivity led to new understanding of atomic structure and to the development of nuclear energy. The evidence for quantum physics was initially subtle and unintelligible until a link between the frequency of electromagnetic radiation and the absorption and emission characteristics of matter was observed. Quantum physics is in some sense not a theory, since it is statistical in nature. Exact predictions of a time-varying nature are not possible for quantum physics, as they are for the theories developed by Newton and Einstein. The recent validation of Bell's Theorem that demonstrates quantum interconnectivity (quantum synchronicity) demonstrates that elementary particles, when coupled and then separated, retain instantaneous knowledge of their coupling no matter where they are. If this "impossible" situation can occur with matter, then something like mind-to-mind connectivity, or any other type of psi, is also possible and could follow principles similar to quantum coupling. Quantum concepts offer a conceptual basis, even if not a theory, for bridging the gap between psi and science.

The uninformed or misguided rationale—no theory—is part of the reason for strong negative reactions to the possibility of psi phenomena. This, and the unscientific assertion that there is no evidence or proof of psi needs to be put into perspective.

No Evidence or Proof

This claim by the critics for discounting psi is not valid. There is sufficient scientific evidence for the existence of psi to warrant acceptance of the phenomena. Multilab research and combined analysis of the results provide strong confirmation. Absolute proof, as for any psychological, social or medical study, is difficult to obtain due to compounding variables that are always present when measuring human performance in any experimental condition. The best case for psi has recently been stated by Dr. Jessica Utts, a leading statistician at the University of California at Davis, CA. Her analysis was part of the independent evaluation effort performed on the STARGATE program in 1995. Her statement: "Using standards applied to any other area of science, it is concluded that psychic function has been well established." Individuals who review the existing psi research data without bias reach the same conclusion, yet the claim that psi has not been scientifically proven or demonstrated has been used effectively to prevent acceptance of psi research projects.

In the early phases of psi research leading to the STARGATE program, I helped design and implement a shore-to-submersible and a submersible-to-shore psi communication project.[12] Remote viewers were on board a deep diving vessel that descended 1,000 feet to the ocean floor. Other remote viewers were on land at the SRI laboratory, in Menlo Park, CA. Results of these remote viewing experiments from underwater to land and from land to underwater at a 500 mile distance were successful. A proposal was prepared for the U.S. Navy to extend this communication project using submarines. However, the secretary of the Navy rejected the proposal on the basis that remote viewing had no theory and had not been proven.

Later, we learned that the likely reason for rejection of the proposal was the concern that any potential form of communication with submarines, no matter how unusual, could jeopardize the chances of having an expensive low-frequency communication system approved. Thus, it was better to deny psi totally for political reasons.

Even though spontaneous cases cannot be offered as proof in a scientific sense, they do provide valuable insight and contribute to improving experimental conditions. These improvements have helped researchers achieve better results while still retaining proper protocol and experimental controls. For example, a friendly experimenter style helps remote viewers feel at ease and relax, an important prerequisite to experiencing psi.

Projects that have interesting and natural material yield better results than experiments that use cards. While those observations may be obvious, some of the early psi researchers tended to downplay the human element. Psi in a laboratory setting can be very subtle and difficult to detect and requires many experiments for building statistical strength. Some individuals respond well to task repetition; others become uninterested. There are many variables that influence the occurrence of psi. There is much that is yet to be learned about psi. Both investigation of spontaneous incidents and laboratory studies are essential if psi is to be adequately understood, more widely accepted, and more reliably applied.

Troublesome Image

Psi phenomena are often judged on the basis of the styles or proclamations of those who claim to be psychic. Some of these individuals link psi very strongly with belief systems or concepts that actually are not essential for accessing the basic phenomenon. If their beliefs are troublesome, psi phenomena may be unacceptable to those who associate them with those beliefs. Sometimes "psychics" do make unsubstantiated claims and are not sufficiently critical in evaluating their own experiences. They may be more interested in media attention than in accuracy or truth.

Media-seeking individuals do not welcome opportunities for psi talent evaluation. Critics and parapsychological researchers share a common interest in challenging such individuals, especially if they are taking advantage of others.

Too Much Value and False Association

Sometimes psi is given too much credit. Occasionally, psi practitioners make claims that they are 100 percent accurate. This is an absurd statement and does not track reality. Psi data can be highly accurate, but this depends on circumstances and how accuracy is being measured. Such unrealistic claims often lead to a rejection of all aspects of psi, not only by critics, but also by those who are curious and are willing to explore the phenomena.

Some critics seek to discredit psi by linking it with topics that have no connection to psi phenomena. They link topics such as "Bigfoot sightings," or "UFO abductions" with psi in order to discredit psi by association. Some critics attempt to ridicule psi by associating the phenomena to irrational or superstitious beliefs. Aboriginal people often linked psi occurrences with superstitions, as they did for other phenomena in nature. While psi may be considered as nonrational— the origin of psi is in the intuitive aspect of our nature—it is not irrational.

Such tactics are certainly easy to recognize and actually reveal a lot about the hidden agenda of the critics using them. Critical evaluation is essential for any endeavor, and many critics have made valuable recommendations on how to improve psi research. It is the emotional skeptic who often receives publicity and can unnecessarily discourage individuals who are curious about psi from discovering what is true or not true.

Fear

Fear may be the underlying reason why many highly vocal critics attack psi. One aspect of fear of psi is that psi seems to challenge the accepted view of reality. When individuals have absolute confidence in the nature of reality as science currently defines it, then anything that does not fit is unwelcome. A rigid acceptance of any world-view becomes an issue of faith. Even though scientific endeavors have led to significant accomplishments and reliable understanding of the physical universe, it is unwise to assume that this understanding is complete. Some individuals accept current knowledge as absolute and consequently feel threatened when their faith in it is challenged. For such individuals, science—which should be an open and unbiased search for what is—becomes scientism and must be defended. Psi phenomena are denounced as something heretical that must be abolished to rid society of nonscientific thinking.

Part of the reason that extreme skeptics often resort to irrational arguments or strategies in their attack on psi phenomena can be an overreaction to early life experiences when they suspected that certain philosophical or religious beliefs were symbolic and not to be interpreted literally. This rude awakening can often instill extreme antipathy toward anything that is associated with seemingly miraculous events. Thus they firmly resolve never to be misled again, and science becomes a new faith. They automatically reject psi phenomena, since they associate them with metaphysical or religious beliefs. Thus, a dilemma: If psi is real, some of the metaphysical and religious material may be valid. Acknowledging psi is for some individuals like opening an old wound. Better to leave it under wraps. Once they have aligned themselves with scientism, the reality of psi poses a threat to their perceived reality base.

A strong commitment to scientism may be more for power than for the altruistic pursuit of truth. It may be a reflection of ego and image. Being on the most popular team is a comfortable situation. If psi were real, knowledge could be obtained through a route other than science.

The existence of psi could also be seen as a direct threat to individualism and independence. People may fear that their secrets could become known, or, even worse, the existence of psi could complicate their lifestyle. The possibility that their thoughts and intentions could be known by others creates discomfort.

Any dissonance caused by the possibility of psi can be pushed aside by aggressively denying the reality of psi. The psychological and psychiatric literature has many examples of how disturbing material can be effectively buried.

No Value

Even when critics acknowledge the possibility of psi, they argue that it is useless; it is not repeatable and has no practical value. This is a totally false perspective—there are no useless phenomena in the universe. Many individuals have been able to develop repeatable psi talents and apply psi effectively; accuracy varies depending on need and motivation. Psi is reliable for many types of applications, as we have seen in Part I. Psi applications in medical diagnostics, archeological explorations and law enforcement are but a few examples. Other possible contributions to scientific knowledge are the subject of Chapter 7, "Delta Regions." The many practical (indeed, potentially life-saving) applications of future-seeing are discussed in Appendix A, "Journaling Your Future." In fact, individuals known to have "good psi talent" are sometimes barred from gambling establishments. Spontaneous cases abound in the literature that demonstrate how psi is useful in the lives of average people.

Healing reported in the literature under various labels—mental, psychic or spiritual—may have resulted from an individual's mobilization of his or her own inherent or latent healing abilities. We are, in fact, continually experiencing some type of healing. Various cells are always at work replacing dying or destroyed tissue or combating viruses and bacteria. Recovery could be an acceleration of an individual's own natural healing system or be spontaneous and apparently beyond self-healing abilities. There are two possible medically related psi applications: (1) diagnostics to determine state of health and the cause of an existing illness or an imminent one—physical or psychological, and (2) interaction to effect or assist in recovery of an illness or injury.

I have experienced and witnessed incidents of where the state of health of others was known through extrasensory means. This information can be obtained from the subconscious mind of the affected individual even when it is not even accessible to their conscious awareness. Such psi-derived information can be for a specific emerging condition and its prognosis. However, with focused intent, anyone can access information about their own emergent state of health— including foreknowledge of conditions in early stages undetectable by medical examination—through mental focus during relaxing periods or through diagnostic dreams.

Psychic healing has had charlatans, and caution must be observed when seeking such practitioners. Some procedures rely on a placebo effect. Unfortunately, the United States does not have a way to license alternative healing practitioners, as is done in the United Kingdom and elsewhere. A simple procedure for keeping track of their claims by follow-up and client interviews would be useful.

Clash of Interpretation

Some individuals can accept the reality of psi, but they resist its potential because of the way they interpret the phenomena. This resistance leads to concerns that prevent them from exploring their psi potential. These concerns are fear-based and need to be overcome.

Loss of Control

This may be a subtle fear that many people have about psi phenomena and is similar to concerns about loss of free will. They suspect that once the "psi gate is open, the flood will begin." They fear becoming confused or overwhelmed, unable to function effectively as individuals.

Dr. Charles Tart, psychologist and parapsychologist, has studied this concern. He conducted surveys of how people would react to taking an ESP pill, or "psi-pill." Such a pill would give them instant psi but at a price—they would not have the ability to turn it off. This pill therefore, offers "omniscience." Under these conditions, Dr. Tart found that no one wanted such a power pill. He proposes that this response highlights the underlying fear of psi that many have at some level. However, his assumption—no control of psi—ignores the reality of real psi experiences, which demonstrate that psi will not surge out of control. We have a subconscious filter or censor that strives to maintain our psychological balance. As long as we maintain this balance, our natural psychic immune system rules. Sometimes individuals do have psychological control problems and may not be able to discern between inner and outer reality. These conditions usually result from some type of imbalance in neurophysiological functioning, maybe from genetic causes or neuronal damage through disease, substance abuse or accident.

Dr. Tart's experiment could be carried out with a hearing pill (hear all sounds) or a smell pill (smell all smells). No one would want to be constantly bombarded with normal sensory inputs. We receive what we need for normal functioning unless we do something that impairs our senses. Psi operates like any other sensory input—we perceive only what we need or are open to perceiving.

Predestination

Some individuals consider precognition (future-seeing) as an indication of predestination and a challenge to the idea of free will. This belief is unwarranted. Precognition is not about an absolute clockwork future; it is about probable futures. Some futures perceived through our psi sensitivities are more likely than others. Predictions of future events with high emotional intensity are easier to remember and are the most likely to occur. The notion of our future as being fixed and final has its roots in ancient beliefs including the belief that "fortune tellers" had true future knowledge. Deductions or inferences from known information may have resulted in some predictions that appeared valid. There may have been instances where valid psi impressions occurred. However, many of such fortune-telling statements were probably fabrications made to achieve some desired response that played on an individual's acceptance of a perceived predestined "fate." Whatever the basis for such predictions, they had little to do with valid precognitions. Erroneously considering precognition as evidence for predestination can lead to a rejection, or fear, of psi in general.

Possession

Some metaphysical belief systems tend to instill a sense of fear about psi phenomena. They profess that psi is facilitated by "beings" or "entities" external to the individual's own personality structure. These "beings" are what bring psi-derived knowledge to the individual. Some psychics are very open about their connection with "controls" or "guides" or some type of entity as the source of their information. Some of these beliefs also include the possibility that an individual can be "taken over" (possessed) during states conducive to psi or at other times during altered states of awareness. Various procedures, including complex rituals, have been developed to protect individuals from the possible intrusion of such "entities."

After intensive study of psi and related fields for over thirty years, I have come to the following conclusion on the concept of guides, entities or whatever name they are given: These mental constructs are not essential for psi functioning, and they may even be a distraction. They may have psychological or metaphysical reality in a subjective domain, probably symbolic, but they are independent of how psi functions. Even if real, these entities must access and communicate through the same psi mechanism that we can access. Eileen Garrett, well-known British psychic, explored the reality of her guides with parapsychologists and psychologists. She eventually concluded that they were aspects of her deep psyche. She shifted from inducing trance states to waking or dream states for perceiving psychic information. Her performance on standard ESP tests was better in the awake state than in the trance state.

I agree with the viewpoint of Laurence LeShawn, New York–based psychologist and healer. He considers guides to be functional entities—they serve a psychological role and only exist at the time the perceptions are received. They may be symbolic of the underlying psi process and presented to consciousness in a form that has meaning to the individual, maybe for control assurance, to provide confidence in psi abilities or for some other purpose. Shamanistic literature has vivid accounts of meeting various shape-shifting entities during Shamanistic journeys. These seem to help the experiencer manage or comprehend the experience in terms of cultural expectations. Another function of these "helpers" may be for ego control. Sometimes individuals can move into psi too quickly and pick up a good dose of ego inflation due to overacceptance of their emerging psi talent, especially if they do not evaluate their psi data realistically.

We usually bring into our psi and other inner explorations much if not all of the cultural belief systems to which we are strongly committed. These beliefs have a significant effect on how we interpret our experiences or how we explain them. For example, someone who has roots in a belief system that holds to a literal existence of evil entities will probably interpret any experience from a perspective of fear instead of simply exploring what is basically there. Sensing of something unknown—maybe unusual electrical phenomena in the brain—can be personified as something fearful and given a corresponding image. Instead of interpreting the unusual experience as an aspect of oneself, one experiences it as something "out there."

Individuals who have a low fear threshold will almost always interpret such an experience as something evil and become concerned about "attacks" or "possessions." In some cases, these experiences of fear may actually be a subconscious signal to alert the individual to first establish a good physical and mental balance, well grounded in reality, before venturing into subjective inner domains. If we are not in balance, it is possible to become too detached and not attend sufficiently to the demands of daily living. No matter how far we explore subjective domains (an opportunity many spiritual and metaphysical traditions offer), we are still rooted in this world. We are here not to escape it but to be a co-creative part of it. We should not forget to "chop wood and carry water."

The concern occasionally raised about the danger of possession if we open up to psi is based on a fear perspective of how the universe operates. When we are in balance and maintain a sense of humor, no disturbing experience can occur. If this were a valid concern, we would all be in trouble every time we "let go" and fall asleep.

Although some people interpret their experiences as negative, these views need not influence in any way those who explore psi from a neutral and balanced approach. Psi is a neutral aspect of the universe. We do not need to distort it into something fearful and therefore lose its potential benefits.

Clash of Use

Some individuals accept psi as long as it is experienced by others. They have difficulty acknowledging that psi is available to them for their own use. Such individuals are prone to seek advice from psychics without checking out the psychic's track record. In a sense, they have given over to others what they are potentially capable of doing themselves. They may also be too accepting of the claims of psychic abilities made by others and may be vulnerable to abuse or dependency. This will continue to be a potential problem until some national or global activity is established that provides evaluation and certification of individuals claiming psi talent for commercial purposes.

Sometimes individuals are drawn into organizations or activities that have leaders who claim to be "gifted psychics." In recent years, there have been instances of fraud by such leaders, and some of these have ended tragically—the mass suicides of Jonestown and Heaven's Gate, for example.

Individuals familiar with psi would not be taken in by extravagant claims from such groups. Throughout history there have been individuals who faked psi talents for some personal objective. As more people understand the nature of psi, there will be fewer tragic incidents.

Occasionally, some groups accept psi as an operating principle that is accessible only to that group. Their purpose may be to impose psychic influence on someone. However, they fail to realize an important aspect of psi's nature—psychic influences cannot be forced on individuals against their will. This error is similar to the misunderstanding that existed for years regarding hypnosis—the condition of focused attention usually referred to as the hypnotic state. While under hypnosis, we will not do anything that is contrary to our own ethical base or our own best interests. There are reliable cases in which someone appeared to be adversely affected by a negative intent from someone at a distance, but such situations can occur only when the expectation and acceptance of this possibility exists.

Some individuals raise questions about the potential destructive effects that our negative thoughts might have, given the reality of psi. There may have been some type of bonding or acknowledgment (maybe through suggestion) that led to such an incident. My view is that as long as we maintain a balanced lifestyle or a firm mind-set to ignore this possibility, then the negative thoughts of others will not adversely affect us through our psi connectivity. The most that could happen under normal conditions is that we might have a hunch, or a dream, about that distant intent. In fact, we want to know! This is like any information source. We observe it, ponder it, and either ignore it or react to it in some intentional way.

Nevertheless we should be cautious. Sometimes our boundaries are pushed back, maybe from fatigue, overindulgences or emotions incited by group dynamics. In some of these intense group situations, psi may have assisted in amplifying the resonances.

A type of consciousness field effect may be created that interacts with those present. Some parapsychology experiments support this possibility. Experiments have been done with sensitive instrumentation, usually sensitive electronic devices, that are placed in large groups. When emotional level is high, certain parameters of the device shift from their random nature, indicating that some type of interaction had occurred. This suggests that our conscious states can create effects that bypass ordinary channels of communication and awareness and interact with material. These effects are weak, however, and are not consciously sensed.

Some individuals accept psi as real and then seek means of developing their psi potential only for their own interests and with intentions of exploiting others. But the belief that psi can be applied independently of how we relate to others is rooted in a misconception; it assumes we have complete control over the process, including how it is directed. While we can activate the process most any time, psi remains a totally subconscious process. Distant intentions of others, even if we subconsciously detect them, would pass through our psi filter unless we had agreed to respond to someone's psi intentions. Our filters would prevent their intentions from having any overt effect on us. Laboratory studies at the Mind Science Foundation in Austin, Texas and other laboratories demonstrate that a remote individual can influence unconscious physiological processes in a designated individual when prior consent has been given. Patterns in certain physiological parameters, such as electrical skin resistance, have been observed to correlate with times of remote intention. A remote individual may imagine the target person to be in a very peaceful place or performing vigorous exercise and his or her physiology responds accordingly. The target individual remains consciously unaware of the specific intention. Even though the statistical correlations are weak, they are consistent and reach levels of significance. These influences are like subtle alerts; they are information only and do not result in any voluntary action. These experiments, generally referred to as "staring" experiments, are repeatable and are well documented.

There are also groups and organizations that accept psi but conceive of the phenomena as only possible with certain philosophical or metaphysical interpretations. Psi abilities in those who do not accept their perspective are not acknowledged and may even be considered as something negative when they occur. This stance denies the fundamental nature of psi. It is universal, democratic and potentially available to anyone. By removing barriers to psi that can result from constricting or elitist perspectives, we are better able to relate to others, and to the co-creative principle of the universe that strives to overcome the walls we are prone to constructing.

Clash of Semantics

Sometimes our confluences with the ideas or activities of others are muddied by the words used in our dialogues. A wide variety of interpretations can exist, depending on background differences and sometimes on the image or association our terminology invokes. Hypnotism, for example—developed from a relaxing procedure by Franz Mesmer in the 1700s—was based on assumptions involving magnetism. This basic idea, known as mesmerism, was popularized in a sensationalist media and led to a public reaction against the technique. Decades later with a new name (hypnotism) and with the understanding that this "state" was a subconscious process resulting from a consent to cooperate, this technique became generally accepted. It can be especially useful in therapeutic practices such as habit breaking and pain suppression. The name change was essential for this new dialogue and acceptance.

Similarly, psi phenomena have a history of semantic issues that had to be overcome. Some of these relate to concepts of how the phenomena occur. Others relate to the image given by some psi practitioners. Part of the semantics difficulty arises when psi is linked with superstitious or occult practices. The development of electromagnetic radiation theory by James Clerk Maxwell in the mid-1800s led to a concept that psi was a result of electromagnetic radiation transmitted to and from individuals' brains. This also tracked growing knowledge of the brain's electrical nature through neuron and chemical activity. Thus, the term *telepathy* (distant feeling) was coined in the late 1800s by British researchers to break away from superstitious occult beliefs. The term *clairvoyance* was also used to describe those instances when individuals accurately described distant scenes not directly associated with someone's knowledge (i.e., no brain was "sending"). But even these terms took on a negative image when "telepaths" and "clairvoyants" were caught faking demonstrations.

In an effort to recover from the negative image that stage personalities and unscrupulous individuals had given the phenomenon, a new term, *extrasensory perception (ESP)*, was coined by parapsychological researchers in the early 1900s and made a household word by Dr. J. B. Rhine through his parapsychological research laboratory at Duke University, starting in the 1930s. In the 1940s, British researchers coined the term "psi" to be more neutral than ESP and to avoid any unnecessary assumptions regarding the sensory nature of the phenomena.

As mentioned earlier, for the STARGATE program and the early research leading to it, physicists Dr. Harold Puthoff and Russell Targ at the Stanford Research Institute (SRI), along with others on the research team, accepted the term *remote viewing* to represent the informational aspect of psi.

Remote viewing came to represent what could be called telepathy and clairvoyance. The early work had a beacon person (potential sender) present, which meant that the data perceived by the remote viewer could have been obtained from someone's knowledge (telepathy model) or from the environment (clairvoyant model). Later remote viewing research projects involved target material that was unknown to anyone, and remote viewing became more closely associated with the earlier concept of clairvoyance.

For most applications, it is impossible to tell if remote viewing information comes from a mind source or from a purely environmental source. In practice, it is almost impossible to set up experiments without anyone present somewhere. A person may not be an acknowledged part of the remote viewing experiment but may be connected at a subconscious level with the subconscious of the remote viewer.

This is why I prefer to think of this phenomenon from a general perspective (psi) and to visualize a neutral concept, like a mind hologram. It avoids possible misleading assumptions about data source or explanatory concepts. A mind hologram could in principle have data from any source—other minds, the environment, or even one's own future knowledge when the target of the psi project becomes known.

The idea of remote viewing has actually shifted in practice, and most practitioners directly or indirectly acknowledge occasions when remote viewing of someone's knowledge is the objective, such as when applied in medical diagnostics to access someone's subconscious knowledge of their medical condition or when locating a hostage. This is, however, a significant shift from the original intent of remote viewing, which was meant to be only of external environments and not of someone's knowledge.

The main reason for retaining the term remote viewing in STARGATE had to do with political and semantics considerations. When

I helped establish the Department of Defense's remote viewing research program in 1976 and took on duties as the government's contract manager with SRI, I chose to keep the term *remote viewing*. It was not too dissimilar from the technical remote sensing work (detectors on airplanes and satellites) for which I was responsible. I knew that terms like *ESP*, *clairvoyance* and *telepathy* carried psychological baggage in my scientific and bureaucratic environment and would create more problems than they were worth. Better to start a new terminology than attempt to put the historical terms into context. This turned out to be a useful strategy. New terms offer a chance to start over, especially if the older terms stir up emotions or biases.

A similar reaction occurred with the early Russian parapsychological research. In the 1920s, Leonard Vasiliev's ESP laboratory was closed because the phenomena he was studying did not fit in with Marxist dogma. Therefore, by definition, it could not exist. Vasiliev recast ESP around a "materialistic" model of electromagnetics and telepathy, and his laboratory was reestablished in 1932. A shift in semantics, along with concepts, was all that was necessary.

Many times the terms we use raise unnecessary barriers in the minds of others. It is up to us to find meaningful and creative ways to overcome these blocks to dialogue so that understanding and discovery can continue.

φ φ φ

There are many types of confluences. Some of them have obstacles set by others; some have barriers of our own making. When we overcome these obstacles and barriers, we can begin exploring our psi nature and discover its potential for ourselves and others. We can interact with smooth and dynamic co-creative streams that eternally flow near the surface of our conscious awareness.

chapter
seven

Delta Regions

φ

In my dreams of the night, I often visit remote rivers. They are small, cascading mountain streams or large, slow-moving rivers that approach a vast ocean. As I explore my dream landscape, I am especially drawn to the places where rivers meet the sea—their delta regions. Here the water spreads apart and forms complex networks. A wide variety of plants and wildlife exists here. The soil in the river is filled with nutrients brought from upstream sources.

As rivers approach the transition from land-constrained to sea-dispersed, they fan out into small channels. These channels branch into smaller pathways and interconnect with one another. Sometimes they travel underneath the porous soil or sand and are not visible. Even though the river disperses into many streams in seemingly random patterns, it is the same river—only the shape or form has changed.

Eventually the currents in river deltas reach the boundary between land and sea, and they are freed from their constricting pathways. The river has not disappeared; it has merged with a deeper reality. But it is a reality that is interactive with many natural processes, and in time the essence of the river returns to its original highland source.

Interconnecting networks in delta regions can be rigidly formed channels that cut through bedrock, or they can be flexible, frequently nudging through soft terrain to create new pathways.

From a distance, the river may give the appearance of being smooth and placid. Up close, we can detect its motion. It may have gentle, flowing currents, or ripples and waves may disturb the surface. Wind, river contour, boulders and submerged rocks create visible surface patterns. Sources within the river—fish, amphibians, animals, vegetation—create wakes or swirls. However caused, these ripples and waves can move across the surface in any direction, with or against the current, even into other channels. These motions are obvious, but we must be close to the river to detect them. We may even need to enter into the river to determine the cause of the disturbance. Even then we may not discover all that can be known about the river dynamics. That may require a microscopic look at a drop of water to learn about the nature of its molecules and atoms. We need to choose what it is we want to observe and select how we make the observation. So what is it we observe when we gaze at the visible and invisible interconnections in a river delta—from afar, nearby or within the water's depths?

It took many river journeys before I realized that river deltas reflect like mirrors. They resonate with delta regions within my own mind and with boundless rivers flowing deep in my psyche. River deltas remind me of other places where transitions or connections occur.

Brain Regions

Since the development of the electroencephalogram (EEG) in the 1930s, medical science has been able to take a peek into some of the complex processes occurring within the human brain. Much has been learned from the measurement of electrical activity in the brain by means of electrodes placed on the surface of the scalp. Weak electrical currents show patterns, or brain waves, and are representative of the brain's neuronal activity. Research has shown that our brain hemispheres are generally specialized. The left hemisphere is associated with linear, logical and verbal functions. The right hemisphere is associated with creative activity that involves detecting patterns and is basically nonlinear. EEG devices are readily available that permit an individual to observe his or her brain-wave activity, for the purpose of achieving relaxed states and for bringing the left and right hemispheres into synchronization, which helps improve intuition and creativity. This shift in brain-wave frequencies is achieved by observing patterns displayed by this biofeedback device and intending the desired result. We can control some aspects of our brain processes.

There are four types of brain waves, each of which corresponds to a particular mental state. The more relaxed we are, the slower the brain waves we produce. When we are awake and active, beta (β) waves, the fastest, are dominant. When we are relaxed, alpha (α) waves are dominant, and when we are deeply relaxed, theta (θ) and delta (δ) waves, the slowest, are prevalent.

Several of these brain-wave patterns occur when we are asleep. After sleep onset, we progress through four stages of brain-wave activity, corresponding to different depths of sleep. Theta waves dominate in the first stage, while delta waves account for 20 to 50 percent of the brain waves seen in the next three stages, with the greatest percent of delta waves occurring in the deepest (fourth) stage. After this initial progression through the four stages of sleep, we return to a near-awake condition known as rapid eye movement (REM) sleep, in which dreams occur. In this stage theta waves dominate, as they do in the first stage of sleep, but in REM sleep the pattern charted by the EEG reflects eye movement activity and has a distinct sawtooth-shaped pattern, which allows this type of sleep to be identified. Over the course of a night, we spend progressively less time in the delta regions of sleep, until we are predominantly in the REM dreaming phase. About 20 percent of our sleep time is in the REM stage. A normal newborn infant spends about 50 percent of its sleeping time in REM sleep; a premature infant has about 70 percent to 80 percent REM sleep.

Researchers associate the low brain-wave frequencies with a quieting of neuron activity. Some yoga practitioners are able to shift their brain waves into the highly altered states of theta and delta to connect with deep aspects of their psyche. Parapsychologists have searched for correlations between neuronal and psi activity during psi experiments and found some evidence for a shift in the alpha frequencies to slightly lower values. Our brain has a natural inner clock that regulates the timing and phase of alpha frequencies. When we shift attention we break this connection, but the cycle quickly resynchronizes. Research in the STARGATE program gave evidence for a synchronization/desynchronization effect when a remote viewer perceived the concealed target. STARGATE research initiated exploratory work that looked for correlations between magnetic components of brain-wave activity and remote viewing perceptions, but firm conclusions could not be made due to equipment sensitivity limitations.

Recent research in the neuroscience laboratory at Laurentian University in Sudbury, Ontario, Canada, has shown that regions in the brain's temporal lobe, especially in the hippocampus and amygdala, may be involved in interpreting psi perception. This pair of almond-shaped structures are principal organs for ascribing meaning and importance to objects perceived in the environment. The hippocampus provides the cognitive framework; the amygdala produces emotional meaning. The psi process may be initially activated in the brain's right hemisphere in the occipitoparietal interface, which is normally associated with visual patterns. This specific brain region may be where psi detection occurs, and if so, it represents the physical link between the brain and the domain where psi resides or is facilitated.

Parapsychological research in 1998 by Kairos Foundation in Wilmette, IL, and the University of Illinois at Chicago, IL, with gamblers has shown that minute fluctuations of EEG signals known as event-related potentials (ERPs) gave evidence for psi. In these precognitive experiments, ERP patterns at times when participants observed the target to be selected were different from times when they observed those not selected. This indicated that, at a subconscious level, brain activity can be a tip-off for the approaching "lucky guess."

In the early 1990s, work in Russia by Yuri Dolin at the International Academy of Human Potential in Moscow found that the amplitude and phase of an individual's alpha frequencies correlated with times when someone was focusing on mentally interacting with that individual.

Recent EEG studies with healers, performed at the Ozark Research Institute in Fayettesville, AR, show that focused mental states conducive to promoting wellness in others lead to increases in delta frequencies. This may reflect a deeper type of dreamlike connectivity than when only shifts in the higher frequency patterns occur during psi perception.

These and other investigations provide clues on how psi interacts with ordinary brain processes. Our brain is a type of river. It has a sequential bit-by-bit flow of neuron activity (the current), it has an overall pattern-making aspect (the ripples on the stream), and it has a myriad of interconnectivity pathways of cosmic proportions (channels). Somewhere within its many diverse functional regions is the interface to other domains—those delta regions that extend throughout the universe, or beyond.

Quantum Regions

Recently, I was asked by Ms. Rhea White and Ms. Suzanne Brown to write an article for their *Exceptional Human Experiences News* publication about synchronicity—the intersection of events in a way that appears to result in a meaningful coincidence. I anticipated writing about a few of my own synchronistic experiences, along with views on the principles that facilitate them. I wanted to go beyond "they just happen." I knew from my studies of quantum physics that it might be possible to cite analogies between synchronicity and some quantum physics concepts and observations. As I plunged into my review, an old concern surfaced—quantum physics and the nature of light are difficult to comprehend.

Depending on how a unit of light (photon) is measured in physics experiments, it sometimes behaves like an elementary (indivisible) particle and at other times like a wave. Similar experiments done with elementary electromagnetic particles have shown that they, too, exhibit this dual nature. But how can this happen? The statement "it happens that way" is similar to saying that synchronicity "just happens."

Some interpretations in physics view the nature of light as a duality—either a wave or a particle, not both simultaneously. Other viewpoints in physics consider the question "What is light when not being observed?" to be a meaningless, ambiguous question. In this view, the true nature of light cannot be determined. The act of observing it (measuring it) collapses its existence into either a wave or a particle—depending on how it is being measured—but not both simultaneously.

Maybe the act of physical measurement does cause a collapse of the light "entity" into a wave or a particle, but might some less intrusive method of detecting (such as via psi) reveal its true nature? Even more, maybe light is not where it appears to be. Maybe light exists as a unity in a deeper domain but can only make its appearance as a wave or a particle in our three-dimensional world. Maybe light is a swirl or vortex (particle) superimposed on a vibrating sea (wave) within that deeper domain. In that region, the particle and the wave are one.

I was happy that mathematics could mimic reality, but I had come to see that the real physics—the basics, the reason for the observable physical phenomena—could not be accessed from mathematics. Mathematics at best could only hope to generate an after-the-fact map of the terrain—not the terrain itself. This was a painful realization, as I had hoped that my forays into academic physics would provide a deeper understanding of physical reality. What I experienced was the opposite; I understood physical reality even less than before and could only shake my head in disbelief. Newtonian physics (the clockwork universe) was nice, easy stuff, and I eagerly applied it in performing orbital calculations for the early Gemini space missions during my aeronautical engineering career. However, Einstein's special and general relativity and quantum physics left me in a state of mental chaos. Could those theories really be true? Of course, as we all know by now, they are not only true (I still think "conditionally true"), but they are incredibly successful. The atomic age and the computer age have transformed the way we live in an astoundingly short span of time. But such fantastic success does not tell us much about the "real" nature of reality. Just what is a spacetime continuum, the "curvature" of space, the "quantum wave function," or light? New developments in physics termed *string theory* may help in understanding the deeper nature of reality. String theory refers to the idea that all reality is based on fundamental vibrational properties of spacetime.

Formal course work on these topics usually leaps directly to the overt mathematics and does not pause sufficiently long on the essence of physical phenomena. Mathematics helps us apply what has been learned about the nature of waves and subatomic particles, even cope with the complexities, but what is behind the veil of formulas? Do formal educational programs make any attempt to capture the real mystery, or is that something we do not want to really face? Are we fearful of the essence behind the physical phenomena that we all take for granted?

In my musings while I was writing that synchronicity article, my thoughts drifted to the nature of light. It exists in potential but not in reality (at least not our conscious reality) until it is measured or observed. Quantum physics thus denies conventional reality to light when it is traversing between measurements. However, Einstein's spacetime geometry does permit a type of existence for light as ripples on the spacetime fabric. When considering "Where is light when it is not being observed?," the two most powerful constructs of reality do not agree. Einstein's model of the universe is continuous, with discrete events amenable to prediction; the world of quantum physics is a sea of probabilities, and specific events are unpredictable. But quantum physics allows for a nonlocal effect. This means that subatomic particles that have been in physical contact with each other retain a "memory" of that connection, no matter how far apart they are. When a change happens in one, the other is affected—instantly—regardless of distance. This *instantaneous* connection, even across galaxies, flies in the face of Einstein's cosmic policeman—the speed of light limit.

Quantum events are puzzling, but equally puzzling is the phenomenon of synchronicity at the personal level of experience. A conjunction of events occurs that has significance and meaning; it is not a random occurrence. Something has nudged us to that place at that time, and we discover what we need to have or know. It is as if we were guided to that encounter. Of all the event possibilities coming our way, something happened that brought two paths together that would not have otherwise met. In that meeting, we discover something important, something meaningful. Personal synchronistic experiences seem to follow a process similar to quantum coupling and nonlocal connectivity. Intentionality is somehow involved in the process. We have a need or desire—whether conscious or subconscious. In the quantum measuring process, the intent is to observe, to know. In the personal synchronicity, the intent is to find or discover— also a type of observation. Maybe at subconscious levels we "observe" all possible future paths or intersections—our event probabilities—and phase-lock (select) one or more when feasible for facilitating a specific need. This causes the potentials to become realized, just as observing the quantum wave/particle causes it to manifest as a wave or particle. The wave function now has had a discrete solution. A specific incident from our event horizon has been selected. The exact trajectory or path is not important; it is only the end point, the intersection, that matters. Our intent, our consciousness, had interacted with the sea of probabilities and phase-locked with a specific one. It is as if a precognitive merging with this possible future event helps bring about the actualization of a synchronicity.

The idea of consciousness having an influence on achieving future possibilities is an extension of the more obvious everyday situation of consciousness interactions. Consider the role of thought in the act of moving an arm. We have a thought: "I am going to lift my arm." Then, "I will lift my arm—now," and we "have" it rise. There it is, waving above our head. How did that nonmaterial thought cause an interaction to start in our brain that in turn caused all the necessary connections elsewhere in our body to "happen"? How did that intention from something—essentially a no-thing—to something specific manifest? Maybe we are too close to the great mystery of consciousness to adequately determine or even sense how we really interact with the physical world. Something creative brings together the imagery that phase-locks, or resonates with, the appropriate regions of our brain. That something seems to dwell in a region outside of conscious reality where it (we?) can interact with our mind-body system as a whole.

Conventional science claims that consciousness (or the illusion of it) is only a by-product, or epiphenomenon, of known processes in the brain—the chemical and electrical activity of all the various molecules and impulse-carrying networks. It is ironic that physics has put the Newtonian clockwork universe into perspective and shifted its philosophy to accommodate the observed reality of the probabilistic and indeterminate quantum world. While biologists, including neuroscientists, still cling to a strictly deterministic perspective of how the world (and brain) must be constructed. Consciousness, in their view, must originate from within the physical constituents of the brain and remain there; its influence must be entirely within the brain. In the microworld of quantum events, consciousness has an influence that extends beyond the physical boundary of the brain. The act of any measurement or observation of a quantum event affects what is "out there."

If the act of observing affects the results of a quantum physical measurement, then the act of observing can also affect biological systems, such as our brain. That is, consciousness (mind) may interact with the brain through an act of "observing"—the link between the idea (to raise an arm) and the act (the arm rises). This may result from a resonance between the idea or thought and the region of the brain that has the counterpart image or other aspect of that thought. But the originating idea may be in a region of the mind that is outside of the brain. The way ideas stir up (connect with) the brain is probably through a quantum-like selection process—call it resonance, wave function collapse, phase-locking or whatever. Such a brain-mind process would have to be nonlocal. That is, the "mind" would not have any conventional physical signal for "causing" the interaction. The interaction process, if it could be called that, is more like a hologram[13] that is continually being rewritten (reformed). But that hologram is not in the three-dimensional world of appearance; it is outside of three-dimensional reality in a region that is essentially wavelike and may be similar to the "waves" we experience as electromagnetic. This region or space would be essentially timeless and spaceless as we define time and space; something like a continuous "now" that is everywhere.

The issue is "How do such regions interconnect or communicate with the brain processes?" That is essentially the problem confronting physicists as they wrestle with the nonlocal aspect of quantum physics. Whatever the connecting principles, something like a hologram would probably be involved, but it would have to be quite different from the hologram we create in our three-dimensional world with electromagnetic radiation.

Some type of connecting principle exists, even if we are not yet sure what it is that is being connected or how that connection actually occurs. Words like "resonance" or "wave-collapse" are only analogies for what may really be occurring. The strongest evidence for such a connecting principle is from the domain of parapsychology and from the effects it studies—our psychic nature and associated psi phenomena. The analogy between nonlocal quantum coupling and psi is too great to ignore. At the very least, psi points toward some type of process that is accessible to our consciousness through an unconscious activity that has a nonlocal character. Psi phenomena show us that the universe is more than three-dimensional reality that can be described from a Newtonian or Einsteinan perspective. Distance and time in psi space are either nonexistent, ambiguous, or structured in extremely small increments that can interact. Psi phenomena should be another data point in our striving to understand conscious reality and the quantum domain. Psi will eventually be given its place in the study of ourselves and our environment. Its existence points toward a connecting principle at the quantum level that interpenetrates or interacts in some way with our material universe. Psi, particularly synchronicity, provides the key for an integrated understanding of ourselves and how our unconscious interacts with others and the environment.

In an interpretation of quantum physics proposed by physicist David Bohm, hidden variables are at the basis of quantum physical phenomena. Ordinary reality, the explicit order, results from activity in a hidden implicit order. The explicit order makes its appearance in the world of reality through wavelike processes. Elementary particles are a result of implicit waves becoming manifest—like swirls on the surface of a river.

In Bohm's perspective, the implicit order projects or injects an aspect of a larger pattern or form to actualize the reality we can experience. It is this process of injection and reinjection that continuously forms and re-forms reality. Reality as we know it does not exist between those fluctuations. Quantum physics only expresses one moment, one observation, and the probability that our observation will be followed by another; it does not explain the connecting process. Bohm's implicit order allows for the possibility of a hidden connecting principle. It is through observations of nonlocal effects in quantum physics and in experiences of synchronicity that this process reveals itself. I suspect that the pathways of the nonlocal quantum principle and the principles of psi phenomena interconnect in delta regions deep within the implicit order.

As David Bohm has indicated, something wavelike continuously fluctuates below the surface of ordinary awareness to create and re-create reality. Similar fluctuations from a hidden domain are continuously dancing on the surface of our psychic streams. We come closest to them at delta regions—the source of our river dreams.

Sometime in the twenty-first century, driven by the findings of quantum physics and continued evidence of psi, a new integrated effort will emerge. It may be called quantum consciousness or a similar term. Evolution of the species takes time; so does evolution of understanding. Consciousness extends or interacts beyond our physical boundaries. What can we do with that knowledge? How will that awareness feed back on itself—for creating new levels of awareness, new capabilities, or something we can currently only imagine or dream of?

Principle of Connectivity and Consciousness Field

When I began psi exploration, I had hoped to discover how to reconcile the phenomena with current scientific concepts, possibly through some type of electromagnetic wave process. It did not take long before I realized that psi is independent of space and time and exists as a separate field or domain. As suggested above, nonlocal effects in quantum physics and the nature of light and its interactive properties in forming holograms offer hints of a process similar to psi, but it may be that we can only continue to affirm psi's reality through empirical observation and our experiences and not clearly identify links to known or emergent physical theories. Physical reality and psi's domain interpenetrate, but their interaction process is unknown and may remain so. We can uncover and apply psi, but as with consciousness, only ponder its roots.

When I first became aware of the psi phenomenon, I explored its practical aspects: What could we do with it? How accurate can psi data be? But there is a greater significance than its utility. The existence of psi confirms that a connecting principle exists in the universe that is an aspect of our subconscious process. It unites all conscious or sentient beings and also links with nonsentient or material aspects of our environment. The existence of this connecting principle has profound implications for science, religion and all of us. This principle is not forceful; many people reject or ignore its existence and consequently do not discover its reality.

This connecting principle is probably wavelike in nature and interfaces, or interacts, with consciousness similarly to the way holograms function. A hologram requires a medium for recording the interface patterns that result when coherent light waves interact. The information contained in the pattern can only be discovered when the hologram is illuminated with the original light frequency. Similarly, this consciousness-connecting principle probably has a wavelike process that can interact with a universal consciousness (or subconscious) field. An aspect of our mind is part of, or can readily access, this field. Its existence is probably in another type of dimension that can interpenetrate with our spacetime physical reality.

Connecting principles describe the physical universe in terms of a field: Gravity and curvature of space are seen as continuous and extending throughout space. Quantum theory sees the field as discontinuous, quantized and consisting of discrete energy states.

It may be that the way a consciousness field and physical field coexist is through a type of quantized or cycling activity. In one instance the physical universe is manifest; in another only the consciousness field exists. Universal principles maintain the structure and reality of both domains.

This field is more than an information storage medium. It may be the root source of some experiences that are usually attributed only to brain chemistry. Feelings such as those described by mystics, poets or others who at times can sense their transcendental nature could be an aspect of this consciousness field. The basis of such feelings would not be primarily from known brain processes; it would result from the connecting principle resonating with certain regions of the universal consciousness field.

The consciousness field probably has several connected layers or domains. One represents what we call sensory information in a type of universal memory; another has feeling aspects; another has creative tendencies or principles and contains forms or templates that provide a type of functional framework for creative or evolutionary processes. Superimposed on all these domains is the knowing part of our experience, the domain where meaning exists. There are other domains that can connect with the consciousness field from other regions of the cosmos or from other dimensions. All of these domains interact via the connecting principle that psi phenomena provide.

This consciousness field may have only existed in potential prior to the emergence of sentient beings. As our conscious awareness increased, and populations grew, perhaps certain domains in the consciousness field also expanded and a type of learning evolved, mostly through trial and error. That which contributed to overall constructive evolution was retained; that which did not was rejected and separated from the positive evolutionary domain of our consciousness field.

It may be that psi has an active role in evolution. The possibility of mind interacting with matter and biological systems suggests that this type of connectivity can also influence an organism's deoxyribonucleic acid (DNA) composition and lead to new adaptations, especially when survival need is critical due to rapid environmental or other changes. Such a mind-evolution interaction process would augment the primary random evolutionary mechanisms that are well established.

Cosmic Regions

The fact that we can connect with others at a distance via psi has significant implications. Spontaneous psi experiences, psi experiments, and especially the STARGATE research and applications activity have shown that psi has an intercontinental reach. No decline effect with distance, as exists for conventional physical phenomena, has been noted. Since psi has an easy time with global distance, why should it not also reach beyond terrestrial boundaries? Why could psi not be effective to planetary locations, even at intergalactic light years? Could we contact, via psi, intelligent beings in or beyond our solar system? Has such contact already occurred?

The ESP experiment from space that Dr. Edgar Mitchell facilitated during the *Apollo 14* lunar mission in 1971 showed that psi had potential for reaching beyond the boundary of earth.[14]

Spacetime, Antigravity and Cosmic Travel

There has been considerable speculation in the science fiction literature and in some technical articles on the possibility of space travel using techniques that achieve speeds close to or exceeding the velocity of light. Limits to the speed of light are central to Einstein's model of the universe.

Developing antigravity devices or somehow "warping space" is perceived by some to permit travel in a region where physical limits are overcome. Mathematical models have been developed to suggest that such engineering, in principle, is not impossible. Some of these concepts develop analogies with tachyons—hypothetical particles that travel faster than the speed of light in certain spacetime regions. However, they overlook energy requirements and do not consider effects on human physiology from the accelerations or time required.

This does not mean that cosmic space travel by some type of space warp is impossible. It is highly unlikely, however, that any progress will be made toward this within the next few centuries. There may be another way to crack the cosmic travel egg. As understanding of the nature of our consciousness field emerges, it may be possible to pursue excursions to other regions of space through a type of "mind-travel." This would not require any physical vehicle, spaceship or body. It would require dedicated individuals who are able to sort our their own personal subconscious material from what may be "out there." A form of remote perception—remote viewing, clairvoyance—would be a nonphysical approach for accessing distant regions of space.

The route to physical cosmic travel may not be from Einstein's spacetime model but from something quantum mechanical. There may be more to the nonlocal connectivity of quantum particles than a potential information-type of connection. (This does not mean that quantum connectivity permits the transfer of information by us. But the particle has experienced something—it "knows.")

There may be a "physical" counterpart to the nonlocal quantum effect. The nature of light (and particles) can be seen as "particles riding on a wave." Could particle aggregates be sent nonlocally to distant places? Emerging concepts in "atomic computers" mimic such a principle. The key to cosmic space travel may not be space warp or antigravity but something like a nonlocal quantum principle that dematerializes and re-forms matter.

This idea would be far-fetched were it not for a simple fact: It happens! In a recent experiment at a physics laboratory at the University of Innsbruck, Austria, a photon was made to vanish at one point and reappear instantaneously at another point a few yards away. This phenomenon suggests that a nonlocal matter wave effect exists that is similar to the nonlocal coupling of particle characteristics.

The evidence for something like nonlocal effects for matter at a macrolevel can be found in the parapsychological literature. Under certain conditions, material objects seem to dematerialize (their elementary particles shift to waves) and then rematerialize at a different location. Such objects have passed through barriers, such as walls and drawers, and on a few occasions have been witnessed in transit, not only in the initial and final position. The conditions conducive to such macrolevel phenomena—usually called recurrent spontaneous psychokinesis (RSPK)—are almost always associated with individuals undergoing mental states of heightened activity, usually a stress of some type. Of course, some apparent macroevents have been faked, and critics tend to focus on these incidents and on explanations involving errors in observation. But not all such incidents can be explained away. The psychological conditions necessary for this type of phenomenon are difficult to produce on demand, although some researchers have accomplished something similar in a long-term structured setting.[15]

The key point here is that a connection can exist between macroscale matter and consciousness, although the facilitating process is not under conscious control or accessible to awareness. Since these situations happen, it is unscientific not to consider the implications and at least begin to develop a connecting model that links mind and matter, even if the specific theory or modus operandi is not in sight. No one can explain nonlocal quantum effects, or what gravity really is. Spacetime per Einstein shifts from one basic unknown (gravity) to another (curvature).

Advances in quantum consciousness research could be achieved during the twenty-first century by linking with the observed nonlocal material transfer phenomena as evidenced in RSPK cases. A considerable amount of cultural baggage would have to be overcome by scientists and by those who might object to such effects on philosophical or religious grounds. The traditional scientist is concerned about image and the implications that RSPK has for orthodox concepts of reality. Some religious representatives also consider RSPK phenomena from a fear perspective. RSPK (or poltergeist phenomena, as this is sometimes called) is seen by some as an aspect of some hidden evil entity and not as a natural but misunderstood aspect of the universe. As nonlocal effects become better known, we can hope to see a lessening of the fear of RSPK phenomena.

The fear that some scientists and certain religious groups have of RSPK detracts from discovery of the deeper reality of this macroscale nonlocal physical phenomenon. As models connecting mind and matter develop, in conjunction with new findings in quantum physics, an understanding of how to achieve "cosmic space travel" may be possible. Physical cosmic travel may not depend on overcoming gravity or warping space but on applying a quantum principle where resonances through mental and technological means are the key to shifting around in local and cosmic domains.

Nonlocal connectivity and potential nonlocal transfer of matter are far shadows of science that can be faintly seen as they drift in our direction calling for new explorations.

I believe that psi contact with intelligent beings in our solar system or beyond is feasible. But there is a significant problem. How would we know if psi contact had occurred?

Some people claim that contact with intelligent beings from other galaxies, or even other dimensions, has already occurred. There are numerous accounts in the media and books of such alleged incidents. The most frequent reports are the so-called "alien abductions."

Individuals going through these experiences say that they are real and that they themselves actually were transported in some unknown way to either a spacecraft or some nonearthly locale. Some of these experiences occur while awake or in a type of dreamlike state. Other accounts were developed from buried memories through hypnotic regression.

I have reviewed many of these accounts and talked to people who claim to have had these experiences. Although no one ever knows exactly what someone else has perceived, I believe that most (if not all) so-called abduction experiences are not evidence of contact with extraterrestrials or other dimensions and that they are not evidence of "aliens" in our midst.

We are usually not given background information in the written or verbal accounts. What was going on in the life of the experiencer prior to the "abduction"? Was he or she going through an intense introspection period? Was there a serious illness involved? Was someone present at that time who expected a UFO encounter? What happened after the "abduction"? Had the experiencer recovered from a serious illness? Did the individual find new life directions and make significant changes in lifestyle? Questions like these would provide a much better understanding of the total experience than is usually possible from the media accounts.

There is one question I would like to ask all abduction experiencers: "Have you ever had a lucid dream?" My hypothesis is that their answer would be "No." That is, they have had no prior experience with lucid or conscious dreams and are unable to place their abduction experiences in a lucid dream context.

I propose that UFO abduction experiences are lucid or conscious dreams. The experience is real but not in a literal sense. It has physical or psychological importance for the individual, probably associated with some inner prompting directed toward lifestyle change, self-discovery or new creativity. Our society's techno-orientation and denial of subconscious realities can significantly affect how experiences from within are interpreted. Tech-talk, such as "spacecraft," "UFO" or "aliens" is consistent with contemporary terminology and society's dominant external orientation. Many people have great difficulty acknowledging that we even have a deep psyche and prefer to project inner experiences—when they occur—onto the external world. The experience was "out there," not "in here." This is especially the case when troubling material emerges from our subconscious.

The UFO abduction accounts do describe aliens. These aliens are the unacceptable aspect of ourselves or of society—our shadows, our fears. In a symbolic sense, UFO abduction and other alien encounters represent our alienation from ourselves—from hidden streams deep within our psyche. They represent a disconnection from our integrative, co-creative sources. When fragments break loose from the murky depths of the subconscious, they rise to the surface, creating unfamiliar ripples that are misinterpreted. They are unrecognized river dreams.

The thousands of UFO and alien sightings over the past few decades argue against them as real events. A long-duration intergalactic journey, even if possible, would require years of traveling at speeds near the velocity of light. Life support and propulsion material for such a journey would require a huge spacecraft. None of that magnitude has been detected on radar that routinely scans the skies. Although unidentified radar data are occasionally reported, these "blips" were likely a result of atmospheric disturbances.

During the 1960s, I had the opportunity to give assistance in reviewing reports of UFO sightings sent or called to Wright Patterson Air Force Base, Dayton, Ohio. My office was next to the Project Blue Book office in the Foreign Technology Division (FTD). Project Blue Book was the name given to the Air Force's investigation into UFO sightings provided to FTD, many through a special hot line. Many of the incidents I reviewed and occasionally helped evaluate were either fraudulent or a clear case of misinterpretation of ordinary phenomena. Usually, when UFO sightings were prolific in the press, any unusual sight was assumed to be a spacecraft—even when it was clearly a planet, a high-flying airplane or unusual cloud formations. There were some incidents that could not be attributed to faulty observations. As I studied them I came to see that many, if not most, were inner experiences that were thought to be "out there." In some instances, the individual had suddenly recovered from a life-threatening illness. A few individuals reported an increase in psychic sensitivities, as would be expected when connections are opened with our inner resources and psi nature. After several years of my informal association with Project Blue Book, I came to the conclusion that the sightings or encounters reviewed—including the previous Roswell incident in 1947—were NOT about extraterrestrial visits.

While most could be attributed to faulty conclusions about something real that was observed, there were those that did point to an inner process at work. They were similar to experiences described by aboriginal shamans. The UFO experiencers had made contact, but it was with their own psychic streams. Like medicine men, or shamans, they experienced a type of initiation. That initiation, steeped in symbolism, was interpreted either literally or translated to consciousness in a form compatible with their cultural beliefs and expectations.

I had the *Mussolini Encounter* (Chapter 1) lucid dream around the time I was beginning my psi explorations. That experience, and several others, allowed me to directly discover how *real* an encounter with our psychic streams can seem. For a few moments during that episode, I was absolutely convinced that the wall had disappeared and that a real person was walking into the room. I felt the impact of the bullets from his gun and even responded by having welts appear temporarily where I "felt" the bullets strike. Had I not later looked at the target picture, I would not have been sure what caused that vivid experience. I might very likely have assumed it was an "entity" or alien attack and not understood it as originating from my dreaming mind. I had in a sense "attacked myself" to vividly convey the content of that hidden picture.

I believe that a process similar to *Mussolini Encounter* occurs when individuals have an abduction experience. In some instances, expectations from others may be dramatized in a lucid dream. In other incidents, abduction experiences are like a Shamanistic journey and have a perception of travel, an initiation and a return.

No one can say for sure why these experiences are numerous. The reason may be linked to our collective unconscious or the consciousness field of society. Something is trying to emerge. The experiences do call attention to our psychic nature and to our universal connectivity. Even though they are usually interpreted from a fear or threat perspective and presented in high-tech symbolism, the experiences may be an early glimpse of the emergence of a new evolutionary stage in the consciousness of society.

In the century ahead, more people will likely discover or uncover their ability to travel between inner and outer realities, and more regions of our subconscious domain will become accessible. Then delta regions of our mind will expand and extend further from the known shores of reality, and we can begin considering new ways of exploring—ourselves and the cosmos. We will join hands with the alien within us and explore together.

At one time I thought that UFO experiences provided evidence of psi contact from extraterrestrial or multidimensional intelligences. The psi process has an easier time with forms, shapes and feelings, much like the usual language of dreams. While logical information such as words and names are accessible via psi, these are not as reliable as psi's pattern-making ability. Thus, if intelligent beings on distant planets wanted to contact us via psi, their approach would probably be similar to that used in NASA's deep-space mission that had symbols inscribed on its space capsule to convey an understanding of planet earth should that capsule be retrieved by a distant intelligence. These were simple pictograms and included forms of humans beings, a circle with the symbol for pi and its numerical value 3.14 . . . and a sketch of earth's location in our galaxy.

Similarly, if psi were to be used in establishing intergalactic communication, the first step would be to get attention. Thoughts through space, for example, would have to be symbolic to enhance reception and understanding. Maybe the best "attention getter" would be to focus on a symbol for distant travel (a spacecraft), for curiosity (inspection), and for themselves (the various intelligent beings). Persons sensitive to such hypothetical communication would automatically interpret the impressions in terms of their own experiences. Memory of science fiction scenarios from the media would essentially mask or significantly distort them. Distinguishing between extraterrestrial messages and memory associations would be extremely difficult, if not impossible.

I believe that a small group dedicated to such a task could succeed in establishing such contact. It would require extensive understanding of subconscious material and the nature of their own psi perception in ordinary circumstances.

Some individuals postulate that extraterrestrial intelligence may have discovered principles that permit "real" space travel through some type of multidimensional access. Others suggest that UFO's are entirely of multidimensional origin. These concepts are extremely fanciful and remain in the realm of science-fiction fantasy. Furthermore, it is unlikely that extraterrestrials having traveled to our region of space would remain elusive. They would want to establish unambiguous contact, as we would to do if we were the space explorer. I agree with Dr. Edgar Mitchell's hypothesis about meeting other life forms who are also exploring the cosmos. They will be benevolent beings who have learned more about themselves than we have.[16] They would have no need for fear and deception—

leftovers from primitive days of early evolution, especially in Earth's domain.

It is unfortunate that some individuals anticipate extraterrestrial contact from a threat perspective. It is also unfortunate that many individuals believe that UFOs have been captured and are part of a vast government conspiracy. Some otherwise reputable individuals even claim that several technological advancements have resulted from information obtained from UFO crashes. Anyone who traces the evolution of technology will discover that there is no current technology that was not theoretically apparent and emergent before the first alleged UFO "recovery" at Roswell, New Mexico in 1947.

There will not be any contact with extraterrestrial intelligences any time soon. That event is probably a long time (maybe centuries) away. Alleged UFO sighting and various type of contact with what is perceived (or interpreted) as of extraterrestrial (or multidimensional) intelligences will continue, but they are *inner* experiences. They have real psychological or inner awareness meaning but are *not* from "out there." We are still very much on our own. It is up to us to continue our evolution on earth and not expect help (or hindrance) from extraterrestrial or extradimensional sources to relieve us of the responsibility. Attributing reality to such perceived contact leads to a philosophy of escapism. "They" will save us or conquer us; or we can blame "them" for causing or contributing to our difficulties.

Similarly, there is *no* government cover-up or conspiracy keeping the "truth about UFOs" from people. What would such a conspiracy serve, except in the minds of those needing a scapegoat for their own difficulties? To believe that such a conspiracy could last through changes in political administrations hostile to each other, or that all governments on this planet can cooperate to the extent of keeping such a secret, demonstrates more faith in government workings than is justified.

There are no captured "aliens." There is no deep, dark, secret place in the U.S. government or any other country's government where the "truth about aliens" is known.[17] There has been no technology transfer from "their" technology. The "aliens" are within, either as symbols of our own subconscious nature or as a disconnect in society or among nations.

There will be many surprises from the cosmos in the century ahead. They will be in the direction of learning and understanding more about the nature of the universe and, consequently, ourselves.

In my view, the current paranoid craze concerning UFO cover-ups and "aliens among us" is a reflection of loss of connectivity with deeper aspects of ourselves. It also reflects the unfortunate tendency of individuals to avoid taking responsibility or to pursue escape routes, rather than to seek constructive and co-creative solutions to the various difficulties of life.

Some individuals already claim to have made extraterrestrial contact by extrasensory means. Until they demonstrate that they have reliable psi talent and that they can distinguish their own expectations from what may be external to them, their claims cannot be considered valid. From what I have seen, individuals claiming to be in contact with extraterrestrials or multidimensional intelligences are more likely "traveling" only as far as their own personal subconscious. Some of their perceptions may convey valid ethical thoughts or metaphysical perceptions, but the information is not from a distant galaxy.

A similar difficulty occurs when individuals believe they have contact with those no longer alive. These experiences are difficult to evaluate, since memory or possibly a psi connection with the memory of someone living may be the source of the experience. However, some of these incidents do lead to verifiable information not known to anyone alive and convey their authenticity through the sense of conviction experienced. If a consciousness field exists that retains all memory, as I believe it does, then given the reality of our psi nature, postmortem psi contact is a possibility. The exact nature of the surviving consciousness cannot be defined; however, some type of region—within a universal consciousness field or a cosmic hologram—may be how individual identity is maintained in a post-mortem state. This region would have memory and feelings. Individuals probably have an aspect of their subconscious mind already linked with such a region.

φ φ φ

Under certain conditions, especially through deep psychic dreams, any one of us can catch a glimpse of hidden domains and their delta regions. For in those regions all connections—terrestrial, cosmic or multidimensional—can potentially occur. As we move through the twenty-first century, new discoveries and understanding in quantum physics, the cosmos and the nature and reach of consciousness will allow us to better understand how vast the connection of external and internal reality can be. For our mind extends through delta regions and links with cosmic streams where new rivers and new *river dreams* begin.

Reflections

φ

Rivers that drift slowly are smooth and seem without time; they have no hurried pace. If we stand quietly and gaze at the river surface we will often see reflections. Sometimes the reflections are mirror images of the distant shore and the terrain beyond or clouds in a river-blue sky. They give us a change of perspective. When our focus is right, we see our own reflection. We wonder who we are, why we came to this shoreline. A small shift here, different actions there, and we would be at a another place on the river boundary.

A face reflecting from a stream may have first stirred our primitive ancestors to begin wondering about themselves. As we stare into our image, we merge with the slow-moving streams—the one outside and the one inside. We wonder about the choices made by ourselves or others that brought us to this unique spot.

The inner experiences that we have when very young have a profound effect on our lives. They provide lifelong motivation and can bring us into alignment with our innate creative energies. It is as if we are born with a template or pattern to help us find our directions. Although such templates may be an aspect of our DNA blueprint and genetic memory, I suspect their origin is in our collective unconscious within a universal consciousness field.

When I became involved with dreamwork and interpretation, I realized that we dream continuously, even when we are not consciously aware of them. We can be in an ordinary dream or lucid dream with a full range of sensory experiences, or we can be conscious in a region where only thoughts prevail. Some type of dream activity probably occurs even when we are awake. Our dreaming mind is a relentless river that is only occasionally illuminated for us to see unless we strive to pull back the curtain that blocks our view.

Dream Gates and Psi

When I opened my dream gate, I quickly discovered that our dream theater can give us insight into personal issues, provide help for problem solving, and enhance creativity. Dreams are sources for physical and psychological well-being, even healing, presenting information accessible through our psi connectivity with others and our environment. As I explored both waking state psi and dreaming psi, I discovered that they come from the same psi source; only their style varies.

Waking state psi can occur through hunches, urges, feelings, thoughts or synchronistic experiences, or through any of our normal senses of vision, hearing, taste, smell or touch. Psi impressions while awake can be brief, or they can be extended in time as in a remote viewing session. Waking state psi impressions usually are hard to interpret, and we often add our own meaning to the perceptions.

Psi in the dream state usually has a mix of sensory modes presented in a dramatic or story-like style. Psi in dreams is usually presented in a meaning context, although it may not be absolute.

Sometimes we perceive psi impressions accurately without knowing exactly what they mean; sometimes we perceive the correct meaning without accurate or even any sensory impressions. For example, we may have an image of a "white sphere" but not know if it is a balloon or a marble. Or we may "simply know" that a certain individual was in an accident without perceiving any image of the crash. Even if we had an accurate image of an accident, we may not know who was involved. There are, of course, variations between these two modes. With practice, as I discovered, psi impressions become easier to recognize and interpret.

Anyone can become receptive to psi during waking states such as relaxing or meditation periods. But people I have worked with in seminars, after being presented with a variety of approaches, prefer intuition and dreams for experiencing psi. Someone who is seeking to apply psi professionally, such as in archeology, police work or medical diagnostics, would probably prefer the waking state. Most individuals are primarily interested in how psi can be of help to them and only need to access psi infrequently. Precognitive or future-seeing dreams are the most significant psi experience for most people. Psi dreams require very little preparation and are "on call" whenever we are sleeping.

For me, exploring psi in the waking and dreaming state is an exciting adventure. Dreaming has allowed me to directly experience creative energies that often have humorous aspects. Their unpredictable aspect affirms that my ego consciousness is detached from the process and that I can expect the unexpected. Our psyche does not need to be considered as fearsome or somber. Humor helps us maintain balance in any activity and is especially important when we explore our inner domain.

I am suspicious of the motives of those who present psi and inner exploration from a somber or humorless perspective. If we take ourselves too seriously, we are at risk of become paradigm-locked, of placing our ego self too much in center stage and distorting or blocking the creative channels we seek to open. When we cut off our creative flow, we also diminish our psi abilities, since the psi and creative processes have similar roots.

Perspectives

My intensive personal and professional exploration into psi phenomena has significantly affected my perspectives about life and the universe we live in. I can no longer consider myself to be a tight little island. Not only do my activities affect others in various direct or indirect ways, so may my intentions. I hold to the view that an evolutionary co-creative principle exists for individuals and society that promotes creative and life-affirming intentions. The major obstacles to discovery of this co-creative principle, including our psi nature, are the resistances and barriers that we erect. When we place them in perspective and overcome them, we become explorers and see their life-enhancing benefits. We become more effective co-creative partners with others and our planet.

We are in a new stream of history beginning with the year 2000. The twentieth century was exciting and challenging, filled with incredible discoveries and racked with human difficulties and world wars. The twenty-first century is ahead of us with opportunities for continuing our transition into a sustainable co-creative planetary society.

Each one of us has a role in this evolutionary process. Assistance is available in the creative streams flowing within our psyche. We can dream *river dreams* to help us meet the challenges of the twenty-first century.

φ φ φ

River Dreams are not far from our waking consciousness. At any time we can begin traveling on their energizing currents. Then we can make new discoveries and uncover hidden talents. They are there as co-creative partners on the river called life.

Afterword

I can only hope that future centuries honor and preserve the wilderness regions of the Earth. For in these wild and natural domains, we discover the patience of nature and sense the eternal processes that drive the universe.

The wilderness, with its ever-cycling rivers and streams, is not only out there—it is also within. When we connect with its natural rhythms and eternal currents, we gain strength and confidence to face the challenges from our journey through life. When we are comfortable in the wilderness, we are also comfortable and in balance with any remote region, including our inner domain.

In the wilderness we can hear the natural harmonies of nature and the subtle murmurs from within. As Robert Frost observed, if we listen quietly, we may discover paths best suited for continuing our journey of discovery.

THE ROAD NOT TAKEN
I shall be telling this with a sigh
Somewhere ages and ages hence:
Two roads diverged in a wood, and I —
I took the one less travelled by,
And that has made all the difference.

—Robert Frost
The Road Not Taken

Journaling Your Future

φ

New River Dreams

Rivers of time have brought us to the beginning of a new century. More than at any other occasion, we pause to reflect on the century past and wonder about the one approaching. Rushing rivers recede toward the horizon, carrying with them a vast array of events that have shaped the course of our lives and will continue to influence our future. Many perceive the past century as being mostly filled with conflicts, with more turbulence to come.

Had we been present at the start of the twentieth century and asked to predict what the onrushing events would be, I wonder how many of us would have glimpsed even a few. Certain cycles were sure to repeat—new discoveries, wars, disease outbreaks, economic upheavals, earth catastrophes. But who would have perceived the approaching atomic age, space age, computer age or the age of global awareness and environmental concerns? Very little advance notice precedes the approaching situation until it surges around the bend, heading our way.

As we pause and gaze upstream, we wonder what is just around the corner, or far upstream, that will eventually be swept close to us or into our path. Will those river shadows, those emerging events, be constructive—individually and collectively—or will they be destructive? If constructive, do we wait passively, or do we take action in the forming of that future? If destructive, is there anything we can do to prevent or avoid the dark shadows? Is our only response to wait and be engulfed by the unfolding circumstances, or can we seek new rivers with new river dreams?

One of the great benefits of being alive at this particular time in the evolution of civilization is that we can have degrees of control of our future. With effort and planning, we already have most, if not all, of what is needed to intersect with the future river that is best for us. These futures are of our own directing; we chart their routes and paddle toward them. There are rivers and their shadows coming our way that we cannot influence or avoid. Unfortunately, some individuals choose to loop anchor chains around themselves and remain immersed in murky rivers from which they cannot easily withdraw.

The personal freedom and variety of opportunities available to us as we enter a new century are enormous. There are many trails that can be followed. But freedom of choice has a downside. There are others who may choose a path that is potentially destructive for us. Regardless of our best intentions and plans, we can become entangled in their paths. Their freedom to destroy, even if they do not perceive it that way, can ripple into our stream, cause a sudden surge, engulf us, or even destroy us. For example, the free choice to drive recklessly might bring someone's route into a collision with ours; a criminal's choice to rob a bank may lead to the sudden death of a guard or clerk. There are countless thousands of examples of how we could be in the wrong place at the wrong time.

The turning point of centuries is an especially fertile time for the publication of predictions and future-seeing. Many people respond to those proclaiming predictions as if they were absolute truths, even when their previous forecasts did not occur. Sometimes their proclamations could have been made by anyone, since the predictions were very general and based on known trends. Some of these proclamations are presented as prophecy, especially if they are very startling or catastrophic—vital ingredients for quenching the media's sensationalist thirst.

Shadows of the Future

What is the nature of the future? Can shadows dancing toward us on upstream rivers be seen before they round the bend? Sometimes yes; sometimes no.

Some rivers are powerful and cannot be avoided, especially if a flash flood from an upcountry storm or a break in an earthen dam occurs. We may hear the roar but not be able to get out of harm's way. Other rivers are gentle with ripples that can be accepted or deflected if so desired. But all rivers are like shadows until they reach the place called now. When they pass beyond now, they only exist in the memory of history. The past is not real and cannot be altered; only its interpretation can change.

The future is not yet actualized and can be changed. It approaches in dancing shadows cast by the waves of probability. Some waves leap high, cast far shadows, and gain strength as currents move them downstream. Their tall shadows are more likely to surge around the bend. Other shadows tossed by ripples are faint and slide between being and not being. The future is not real, but it does exist in emergent or cycling possibilities until it happens and flashes into the place called now. In an instant it passes by and is frozen in the memory of time.

Considering time as only *now* is a commonsense viewpoint that is consistent with experience. Some explorers of the mind, such as poets and mystics, perceive time as an eternal now. There is no future time and no past time. We cannot travel to them to change "now." However, some science fiction writers portray the past and future as something tangible with a life of its own. Some psychic sensitives claim to be able to access real pasts or real futures by means of "time travel." Time can have various meanings, such as psychological time or the slowing of time in strong gravitational fields, but it remains as real only when it is *now*.

We can learn from the past and adjust the directions in which we are going. But can we also learn about the future and adjust our path? Can we perceive the shadows borne along by waves of probability that are approaching us? Can we take action now to better respond to them or avoid them should they actually make it around the bend? Can we tell the difference between very likely events and those that are only possible?

There are two types of possible future events that we can experience by conventional means: those involving interactive dynamics of people and other sentient beings (pets, wild animals) and those involving interactions with our environment (earthquakes, floods, mechanical mishaps). Of course, some potential future incidents may invoke both, such as an automobile or airplane accident resulting from a combination of driver or pilot error and equipment failure.

At a personal level, there are many ways of having future possibilities become very likely, even reasonably certain. We can predetermine many of them through intention and planning. For example, we know or decide when to arise tomorrow morning. The future possibility of arising at 7:00 A.M. becomes actualized when 7:00 A.M. arrives and the alarm rings. We may not leap out of bed exactly at 7:00 A.M., but at least we have the opportunity to do so. But if the alarm malfunctions, then that future possibility does not occur. Our expected future can change or not occur whenever unexpected situations arise from events or the unknown intentions of others. The chain of cause and effect can be extremely complicated, especially when we consider all possible interacting effects from intentions and decisions within social structures and nations.

Those of us who have been involved in forecasting trends (as I was for many years) are painfully aware of the difficulties inherent in making any prediction about the future. We may study trends and cycles. We may estimate the potential impact of new research findings, even anticipate breakthroughs. We may even consider the role of economics, politics, consumer reactions, or a variety of national or global factors and still not derive a very accurate portrayal of what is likely to happen five to ten years or more in the future.

Some general patterns may repeat. Some of our forecasts may prove to be on target. There is no guarantee that specific situations will occur as predicted based on the best data and analysis methodology available. It may be that traditional methods of forecasting need to be augmented, or replaced, by newer analytical methods such as those derived from chaos theory (for example, the models of nonlinear dynamics inherent in dissipative structures). Yet, even these cannot adequately account for the unpredictability of human choices and decisions. While some aspects of our decisions and choices may be easily predictable—the advertising industry has a good handle on that—other aspects of why we do what we do are not within the grasp of external manipulation. It is often the intangibles, the unpredictables of human nature, that cause a sudden shift in the predicted trends and alter future expectations

The other type of possible futures coming our way—those arising from nonsentient sources such as natural disasters and the weather—are equally difficult to predict, if not more so, than possible futures from human interactions. Some general trends may be well known and repeatable—the average temperature at any area in a given month or the cycles of location of most earthquake activity, for example. But sudden and unpredictable situations can occur with little advanced indication. A huge global database, along with complex computer models, may at best only yield refinements in the general patterns and still not be able to predict with any degree of reliability the next hurricane or tornado or the precise time and place of the next major earthquake.

No one is completely immune from any of the geophysical surprises that the future has waiting for us. Even if we live out of harm's way, we can still be affected indirectly by providing assistance to those who are affected. We respond to alerts at the first indication of a forming hurricane or when the strain gauge is off-scale at a geophysical fault line. But before the first signs occur, there is not much we can do, at least not through conventional means. So the question of what possible futures are coming our way is extremely complex. But we can be prepared for the unexpected.

It is possible to "future see" through our psychic sense of precognition. We need to keep future-seeing in perspective and not lose sight of its *probabilities* nature. If we assume that the future is fixed and pre-determinant, we relinquish our free will and ability to alter the perceived incidents. When we view the future as possible but not absolute, then we have the freedom to respond as best as we can—with all our abilities.

The concept of futures as a sea of probabilities is similar to what quantum physics reveals about the nature of quantum events. They cannot be determined precisely; they only exist as a range of possibilities until they actually occur and are observed, as discussed in Chapter 7. The underlying processes are unknown, and only general statements can be made about any condition or state not yet actualized.

A way of conceptualizing how precognition or future-seeing can occur is to consider all types of consciousness to be part of a universal consciousness field that has a holographic-like aspect. This field records all past and current knowledge and future intentions, which is similar to the way our mind actually functions. It has the capacity to integrate intentions from all possible sources to form a probable futures hologram. Anyone can access this future-seeing hologram. Probable futures of personal significance are easiest to access and interpret correctly. This hologram is constantly revised to reflect changes in intentions or situations.

I envision an additional future-seeing hologram that specializes in recording nonsentient events, such as earthquakes or mechanical failures. Information in this hologram may originate from knowledge, liminal or subliminal, in the minds of sentient beings. It may also have a nonsentient source of knowing, perhaps from connection with hidden variables or nonlocal effects that reside in the delta regions of quantum physics.

I believe that any one of us can access this future-seeing hologram. We can perceive those distant river shadows well in advance of their arrival. Not all perceived events will occur; something unexpected can occur after our perception that lowers the event's probability or even dissolves it altogether. As we seek frequent future-seeing updates, we can sense when such probability shifts have occurred. For that is the value of future-seeing: We can ponder the consequence of the approaching incident and then develop strategies to accept, avoid or prevent the occurrence.

Journaling your future is an approach for accessing future-seeing potential. The demands of the century ahead require that more individuals open up their intuitive and psi nature and especially their future-seeing talents. Proficiency in future-seeing can make lives more efficient and can even be life saving.

Journaling Your Future

The best source for knowing what future possibilities are coming your way is *you*. We know from our planning and intentions what is likely to occur in the days and weeks ahead. We can, as most of us do, set a variety of goals for both great and small activities that we strive to achieve. Writing down our major goals in a diary or journal and doing what we can to achieve them is one of the basic activities for helping us reach our objectives.

Another activity, future journaling, chronicles anticipated futures—those that catch us by surprise, for better or for worse. You are the author of this journal. It is the result of your own intuition and psychic scanning of futures that are still hidden from normal sight but are nevertheless heading in your direction. Some of these will intersect with your path; others will be deflected but still come close. Journaling your future allows you to be a step ahead of approaching currents, improving your efficiency, avoiding unfavorable incidents, and anticipating joyful events. Chart your own course in life, uncover hidden aspects of your personality, discover new talents. There is nothing to hold you back from starting and continuing a journal of your future. It is challenging and it is fun. It is also a creative adventure.

When you begin to see the benefits, you will wonder why you did not start earlier. Journaling is not a labor of work; it is a fruit of love, the essence of discovery and living.

The evidence for future-seeing is strong. Highly structured laboratory experiments in precognition—describing a target place, picture or computer response to be selected in the future—have been repeated successfully in several parapsychological laboratories. Hundreds of validated spontaneous cases exist that show clear evidence of foreknowledge through extrasensory perception (ESP). Many individuals have published the results of their independent investigations into their own future-seeing (precognition) abilities. Precognition talents will increase in the future as more people begin serious exploration of their intuitive and psychic nature. The best case was made by parapsychological researcher Dr. Louisa Rhine, who noted that most spontaneous psychic experiences are precognitive. If nonsystematic spontaneous situations are potentially useful, consider the increased utility that would result from purposefully seeking and journaling information on your approaching futures.

Setting the Goal

As with any activity, any venture, you need to decide to do it. You must be willing to begin your future-seeing journey. Although not absolutely necessary, preparing a special journal for your discoveries will greatly enhance your progress. As you journal, you are sending a strong signal to your subconscious that reinforces your intentions. You are demonstrating a clear and strong interest in learning a new skill.

It is best if your future journal is a dedicated notebook or something similar. This is your special document. Therefore, your first action is to purchase, or make, whatever kind of journal you feel is appropriate for the journey you are about to begin. Title it something like *My Journey into the Future*, or simply *Journal of the Future*. Enter "Day 1" (date) on page 1, and off you go. While you are in the mood, attach a photo of yourself on the inside cover. After all, you are the "target person."

Preparing for Your Future

Before embarking on your first future-seeing adventure, you may need to do some preliminary activities. The extent of these depends on what you have already discovered about the reach of your subconscious mind.

If you are just beginning experiences with inner realities, you may want to devote some time to one or more types of exercises that give insight into your subconscious nature. The best, and easiest, is to set aside certain periods for quiet relaxation or meditation, or to begin dream recall. Other activities that help establish or enhance links to your subconscious processes are practices that enhance creativity, expand subliminal sensitivities, or improve intuitive awareness. For example, try switching hands when sketching. People who are ambidextrous seem to do better in psi tests than either left- or right-handed individuals. You may wish to begin with exercises that focus on psychic perception, since that is the basis of future-seeing.

If you have not already done so, participate in a creative act—constructing something, painting or sketching, dusting off that old buried musical talent, or just listening to inspiring music or reading poetry. Being creative activates the nonlinear pattern-making regions of our brain and assists in achieving a balance between the left (logical) and the right (artistic) brain hemispheres. This type of hemisphere cooperation is a form of unity—an important aspect for any type of psychic connectivity, including future-seeing. Being creative brings us into direct contact with a co-creative principle accessible from within.

Improving subliminal sensitivities promotes inner awareness. Even though normal sensory modes are externally directed, devoting attention to what you see, hear, taste, smell and feel can alert you to the subtle impressions originating from your intuitive and psychic nature. By enhancing your subliminal sensitivities, you become more alert in routine activities.

A good way to improve subliminal perception is to selectively focus on one aspect and strive to perceive everything that is possible. For example, walk to a park or look at a building. Focus on one small area and take inventory: What is there? Hold every shape, form, color, motion in mind for as long as you can. Listen to every sound, no matter how faint, for as long as you can. Do this several times a day. Before long, you will automatically take notice of aspects in your environment that no one else detects. You will be able to find lost objects more quickly and even avoid traffic mishaps.

Improving your intuition is an excellent way to help open up your psychic sensitivities. Some aspects of intuition result from the pattern-making abilities of our right brain hemisphere and our subliminal awareness. We may not have consciously noticed when we dropped our house key, but on impulse we walked to the place where it lay hidden, surprised that we found it. Simply being more alert improves our intuition. Intuition has another aspect—it includes information from our psychic perception. Thus, some intuitive impulses are not from previous knowledge or even from subliminal perception—they include information obtained psychically.

There are a variety of ways for uncovering or improving the psychic, or psi, part of intuition. Set up simple exercises like "guessing" the color (red or black) of cards chosen from a deck of playing cards. Attempt to determine something about a friend or acquaintance (with consent) that you have no previous knowledge of and that cannot be deduced by ordinary means. Work with a colleague on a variety of intuition development projects where the objective is to identify the unknown issue.

You may have a hunch or feel an impulse about something, like a fleeting thought. Usually in these types of experiences, the first impression, no matter how vague, is correct. At one time, intuition was associated primarily with hunches or feelings. The ESP research approach using cards with five different symbols, made popular by Dr. J. B. Rhine starting in the 1930s, was primarily an intuitive process, since most of the time participants responded to hunches. They sought no specific imagery, only a "feel" about what the hidden card could be. In the past few decades the term *intuition* has been used by "intuitives" to include impressions that correspond to all of our sensory modes of perception. Some intuitives perceive images, hear sounds, or experience tastes or smells associated with the unknown situation. Thus, there is a clear overlap with what others would label "psychic," such as telepathy, clairvoyance or remote viewing. The distinction between what is intuition and what is psychic is more an arbitrary definition than one of any real difference. This is why intuition development is so effective for psychic or psi development. The types of applications may vary greatly but not the basic modus operandi.

If you want to explore psi from the approaches developed in the recent parapsychological research activities, there are several possibilities. The two most recent are remote viewing and "ganzfeld ESP." Ganzfeld ESP, or "uniform field" ESP, was a term coined by researchers at the Maimonides Medical Center, Brooklyn, NY, in the 1970s. Both terms are based on an awake state approach to perceiving psi impressions. As we have seen, remote viewing usually refers to an alert or slightly relaxed approach. The Ganzfeld technique is a moderately or deeply relaxed state. In the 1960s, the Maimonides Medical Center also explored "dream telepathy" that sought psi in the dream state.[18] Dreams that accurately reproduce a previously unknown distant scene illustrate that remote viewing can also occur in the dream state.

You can use the approaches of parapsychologists to explore psi potential or find some other way. But you must be absolutely certain that your impressions cannot have been anticipated or inferred. As an example of remote viewing, have a friend visit a place or look at a photo that is unknown to you. While he or she is observing that scene or picture, focus on perceiving any impression of what that scene or picture may be. After you have recorded your impressions, compare them to ground truth. Do this until you see evidence of psi contact. Similarly, you can focus on having a dream about that place or picture. Or you can try both approaches to see what works best for you.

In addition to proactive ways of enhancing your intuitive/psi nature, you can improve sensitivities by maintaining a balanced lifestyle with a positive outlook, keeping a sense of humor and avoiding overindulgences. This causes fewer internal distractions and frees more energy for facilitating the subtle processes necessary for psi perception. There will be less distortion in your impressions.

If you already have frequent intuitive or psi experiences, begin your future-seeing journeys at any time. Future-seeing, or precognition, is only one facet of your basic psi nature. Explore your future in a relaxed or meditative state, in the dream state, or both. Even if you have had little or no clear intuitive or psi experiences, you learn future-seeing by doing it.

Setting time constraints makes evaluation of impressions easier. Your confidence in the psi process increases when your impressions correlate to events in the near future. The longer the time interval between impressions and a correlating future event, the harder it is to be sure the incident was not due to chance. When the foreseen event is unique with very specific information, then you can be reasonably sure that it came from your future-seeing ability and was not a random coincidence.

As you gain experience, the accuracy of your impressions will increase. If you feel that an impression is too general, you can seek clarification in a follow-on future-seeing period.

As you work with future-seeing, you will discover that little preparation is necessary. Impressions of the future will occur at any time during relaxation or in sleep during dreaming. The more important impressions are, the more likely it is that they will break into conscious awareness.

You will discover that your intuition improves and that synchronistic experiences occur more frequently. Synchronicity is like "unconscious future-seeing." Keeping a steady interest in future-seeing activates all aspects of our psi potential. Our subconscious mind is always searching and scanning; it seems to know what is approaching and moves our paths (or the paths of others) into a meaningful intersection. Synchronicities, or meaningful coincidences, are one way our psi abilities manifest. Future-seeing and synchronicity have a lot in common. You may not have perceived that future in advance, but when synchronicity happens, there is an uncanny feeling—something like déjà vu—affirming at some level that you knew what was approaching.

Initiating the Process

When you decide to take a peek at your potential futures, set aside a specific time and commit this to only one purpose: future-seeing. For example, if you choose a relaxed/meditative approach, select a time of the day when you can be undisturbed for at least half an hour. Initially, select a specific day of the week when you are naturally more relaxed than at other times. When you begin, keep your schedule simple. One future-seeing period a week can be sufficient, although you may eventually settle on a different pace. Objectives can be general or specific.

During the day of your first future adventure, write out your objective: "I desire to receive information of an event approaching me from the future." Your first future request should be general and openended. Start with perceiving anything that is coming your way. Do not put constraints on your natural psi scanning abilities. As you gain experience, include objectives with a sharper focus. "I desire to receive information of an event coming my way that is highly significant." Such events do not occur often, but when they do, you will be alerted ahead of time. Experiment to discover the best way of setting your objectives—these are individually unique.

In summary, to initiate your future-seeing process:

- *Set Goal:* Throughout the day prior to your future-seeing experience, occasionally focus on your goal of future-seeing.

- *Write Your Objective:* Write out your future-seeing objective in general terms. With experience, change the focus of your objectives to be more specific.

- *Set Time Frame:* As part of your future-seeing objective, intend to perceive only near-term incidents, a week or a few days ahead.

- *Intend Specifics:* As part of your future objectives, intend to perceive unambiguous and clear perceptions.

Perceiving Your Future

You are now ready to meet your future. Relax and enjoy the journey. Here are some situations you may meet:

If you choose information of any future event of interest as your first future-seeing objective, you may have waking impressions or a dream of receiving something unusual in the mail. The next day your mail may have an item that resembles the impressions you had during your future-seeing period. Perhaps you will have a dream of a mountain vista that you do not recognize and shortly afterwards receive a postcard with that scene from a friend you did not know was traveling. You may have a waking impression of a face you recognize to be an old acquaintance and the next day receive an unexpected call or letter from that individual. As you explore your future-seeing potential, you will have many experiences like these. Even though of minor significance, they are part of the future landscape and add confidence to your future-seeing abilities. Then when something highly significant occurs, you will have more trust in your abilities and be more likely to respond appropriately.

If you have been focusing on the objective to perceive "anything significant," and your inner vision presents you with an avalanche scene, you need to consider it carefully. If you were planning a skiing trip, it would be prudent to take extra precautions or even delay your trip. If you had not been planning a skiing trip, an avalanche scene might appear in the news headlines within the next few days at a place of special interest to you. Even though the event is not "real" to you, it is real in the sense that it was part of your informational future at the moment you learned about or read of the event. If you want to restrict your future-seeing to only direct personal experiences, write that as part of your future-seeing objectives.

One beneficial aspect of future-seeing is in perceiving incidents that help you prepare for unpleasant information. For example, a friend may have been (or will be) in an accident and you will be better able to respond to the bad news. Even if the incident has already occurred, you may not receive confirmation of it for a few days—thus it is a future information event for you. Suppose you had a dream of being mugged at a bank ATM, and you planned to go there the next day. In this case, it would be prudent to be extra careful or go at another time or to another bank site. This is the type of impression you can act on, and it may be life saving. The future is a sea of possibilities. You can accept or can act on your future-seeing impressions to alter the probabilities if desired. Remember that precognitive impressions and dreams represent probable futures, not absolutes. Something may occur after the future-seeking session that alters the approaching future. For example, someone intends to visit you without advance notice, and you perceive that intention. That will likely occur, but if the individual has a flat tire or car accident, the intended future may not happen; thus, your dream or impression about the approaching visit may not appear to have been precognitive.

Another example: During a future-seeing period, you suddenly perceive the face of an individual who appears sinister. In a few days you meet someone who looks like that and who is approaching you for some type of business venture. Check the situation carefully before proceeding and act wisely.

Sometimes people resist the future-seeing of significant events because they feel that knowledge of them creates emotional stress or anxiety. It is up to you to what extent you are open to these types of futures. If the news is potentially distressing, you will learn of it anyway. But in most instances, we only perceive what we can reasonably handle; our future-seeing process will present the information accordingly. For example, a friend's accident might be presented in a symbolic way. We receive a vague idea and are spared the emotional impact. My personal view is to be open to all futures. Why run from them? We may perceive an emerging troubling situation that can be avoided. I suspect those of you in law enforcement or dangerous military assignments would readily agree.

Not all future-seeing need be of totally unexpected, out of the blue events. We can also seek futures for situations that we have general knowledge of but that have uncertain outcomes. Future-seeing has the potential for providing an alternate view to what we anticipate from emerging situations that we have set in motion. For example, you are about to close a business deal. Are all the agendas known? Is there something you should know that has not been made clear? In such cases, a future-seeing objective could be: "What should I know about this action I am about to take?" A similar question can be posed regarding an emerging relationship. "Is there anything significant I need to know about _____?" As you gain experience in future-seeing, these are types of questions (objectives) to present to your "future seer."

As your proficiency increases for getting to the essentials, to the basic truths (as psi does), you are better prepared to respond to the variety of approaching situations—those out of the blue and those you are setting in motion.

Assessing Your Impressions

Assessment is essential to future-seeing. It is one thing to have impressions that are, or may be, valid snapshots of the future and quite another to know what to do with them. Gaining experience in evaluating impressions makes it easier to understand and use the information they provide.

Future-seeing impressions vary widely. They can be symbolic, literal or some combination of these. They may be simple or complex. The situation depicted may be personal or impersonal, neutral in emotional content, or highly charged. Incorrect information may be mixed with correct.

The first consideration is the reality of future-seeing. You need to be reasonably sure that the impressions you receive during your future-seeing periods (waking or dreaming) are in fact showing evidence of this phenomenon. Keeping good records (your future journal) of impressions received during different future-seeing periods helps to do this. When events unfold in your life, you will soon know if your door to future-seeing has been opened. Some individuals find evidence after only a few future-seeing periods. Others may require months or longer before traces or shadows of the future can be seen. It is my personal and professional experience that almost anyone who is motivated and has patience is able to open the future-seeing gateway.

You may find it necessary early on to select which future-seeing mode works best for you—relaxed state, dream state or some other—although you can keep open to more than one approach.

If you prefer the awake relaxed state, you need to guard against the intrusion of expectations and previous knowledge. Remote viewing research clearly shows that we can be our own worst enemy and are prone to interpret the impressions too quickly. It is absolutely necessary to record or sketch only the basic impressions—images, feelings, sounds—without interpretation at the time the impression is being presented. Fortunately, our accuracy rate increases when we are working with our own personal material. For example, a fleeting impression of Aunt Jane is likely Aunt Jane. However, we may guard against threatening personal information and hence distort it or present it symbolically. By working with future-seeing, you will come to know your "signature"—those aspects you do well on, those you distort or fail to recognize.

The biggest concern is not so much with perceiving your specific futures but with those cases where you perceive aspects of yourself that are symbolic. For example, if you are recovering from an illness and during a future-seeing period perceive intense earthquakes, odds are your physical trauma has intruded and distorted your impressions. You could not "get away" from yourself. This type of distortion is especially prevalent among people who have become sensitized to millennium fever and are caught up in symbolic aspects of potential changes that are psychological in nature. A projection to external reality occurs, and inner and outer reality are blurred.

Working with dreams usually avoids the quick-to-analyze tendency experienced during waking future-seeing periods. But it also can have distortions. Dreams are primarily dynamic storytelling experiences, and by their very nature mix a variety of literal and symbolic content together. Like highly emotional waking state impressions, they often overdramatize to catch our attention and make a point.

Familiarity with dreamwork allows adjustment for many of the potential distortions that might be in your dreams of the future. Practice and setting firm intentions to have only realistic dreams greatly minimize potential distortions that might occur in the free-flowing nature of the dream state. Dreams are much better suited for probing relationship issues, since the conscious awake ego self is almost always barred from our dream landscape. As you gain dreamwork experience, you will see that certain aspects of any future-seeing dream—the sudden shift in context or action, the intrusion of any attention feature (for example, a spotlight), or the ending—are where the most accurate data reside.

Recording the basic impressions during your future-seeing periods and waiting for confirmation within the established timespan will show your specific patterns and preferences. In time, the distortions will lessen, and the accuracy of your impressions will improve. Be sure to keep good records of the actual events. Update your journal, showing how the real event correlated with your impression.

If your future impressions were of an incident reported in the media, attach a copy to your future journal pages. You may want to keep a separate folder with backup information. This material will be extremely useful for review and analysis. But most important, it offers proof that you are tracking into the future, into the domain of psi.

You may find it useful to share some of your impressions with someone. Then when the event actually occurs, it will be easier to verify. This may be important later on, especially if you plan on presenting any of your impressions publicly.

Planning Responses

As you gain confidence in your future-seeing abilities, you can begin to annotate in your journal what type of response is to be considered. If the impressions seem to be of routine incidents, then simply await developments. Such incidents, though minor, do reinforce credibility and are great learning opportunities. If the impressions are significant in some way, then mark them as an "alert." Maybe no action by you is warranted, but the information will help you be better prepared for the approaching incident. You may have an impression of a friend's sudden illness and be ready to help or call to offer assistance.

The most significant value of your futures journal is your perceptions of future incidents that may require a response. These "ACTION" perceptions may involve you, an acquaintance, or strangers. If they involve you, then carefully consider avoidance strategies if the situation is undesirable. Check your car if you perceive it having a mechanical failure. Be sure to survey your home or apartment if you have burglary impressions.

If the "ACTION" perception is about someone else, you will need to proceed cautiously. You must use tact in relating your future-seeing impressions to others. Many individuals respond negatively to any intervention. Try to develop an indirect approach. For example, you dream of a friend being in a car accident. Find a way to have him or her pay more attention while driving in the days or weeks ahead. If you perceive the situation to be very serious and have specifics (e.g., the accident occurs during an upcoming vacation trip), then you may need to be explicit in explaining exactly why you are concerned.

If the "ACTION" perception is about strangers, such as a possible airplane crash, there is not too much you can do at this time. Maybe in the decades ahead, it will be easier to have disaster premonitions acted upon. Keeping good records is the first step toward achieving this significant potential application of future-seeing.

Continuing the Journey

As you progress, you will discover that "future-seeing" can be achieved at almost any time it is intended. Sometimes, perceptions of the future will occur spontaneously. You may respond to a meaningful emerging future through intuitive actions at times of great stress or danger. You somehow "knew" how to avoid that hidden assailant; you altered your travel plans and then learned of a mishap that could have affected you.

With experience, you will be ready to extend the timeframe of your perceptions from a week or less in advance to several weeks or even longer. This allows glimpses of significant issues emerging in social, national or international events that directly affect us. Since *all* futures are probable futures, the further you seek ahead, the less confidence you can have in the perception. When you perceive something meaningful, set aside frequent periods for updates. The approaching event may become stronger or weaker; you may sense whether the potential incident is becoming real or fading away.

Most of the time, the value of future-seeing is for the immediate timeframe. The perceived events are more likely to happen, and you have some flexibility in responding if need be. Even though a major part of future-seeing is actually of routine events, these are like a car tune-up, or practices. They prepare you to catch those bolts from out of the blue that may be ready to strike at any time from just beyond the range of ordinary knowledge and awareness.

The essences of future-seeing are creativity and survival. By developing the art of future-seeing, you are better able to navigate through the difficult journey called life.

Bon voyage.

The Creative Journal: Journaling Toward Goals and Well-Being

φ

We have the ability to direct our future. Our choices, especially as adolescents, have a huge effect on the path we travel through life. In some instances, our course is significantly affected by situations beyond our immediate control. In others, it remains undefined and awaits our creation. Unfortunately, many individuals make choices early in life that set their path heading in difficult directions, or even toward a dead end. The potential within them becomes greatly diminished. Even then there is always the possibility, with new directions and vision, for shifting to other paths that allow them to discover the hidden resources that are available from within. Ultimately, what we are heading toward is up to us. Even in restrictive environments, the way we respond—our attitude, our interpersonal effectiveness—is always within our control.

The paths we develop or choose, as most of us will discover or have already discovered, have many side trails. Some are filled with distractions. Others connect us to hidden dimensions within ourselves, and to others. Some of these branching pathways link us to unsuspected sources of creativity that propel us forward. As we become more comfortable with our inner nature—our co-creative process—we gain a different type of vision; we can see in-side and out-side. We can learn to be effective in the external reality surrounding us but not necessarily belong to it completely. Our paths in life track on two levels: the surface level that twists along with many obstacles and the wide and deep subsurface level that provides vision, motivation and courage along with insight on how best to proceed along the surface trails.

There are many approaches for selecting, or striving toward, future objectives. Sometimes we can plan general directions fairly well; other times not. Sometimes we drift and permit surface currents to carry us. At any time we can plunge a rudder deep down and catch powerful subsurface streams that help us cut across channels and overcome obstacles. The choice is ours. Anyone can access these creative currents and move toward new directions. Setting goals may not be sufficient; your physical and psychological well-being also have a significant effect on how you navigate through the turbulence that may be between your path and the distant goal.

As you progress toward your goals, you will encounter insight from your psi nature. Drawing on your creative energies brings you into contact with psi streams that are ever present just below the surface of conscious awareness. Information gained from accessing your psi talent can provide confidence in specific choices or the timing of important activities.

Literature abounds with techniques and activities for maintaining good physical and psychological health. We are all aware of positive thinking, goal setting and similar concepts. The trend toward alternative and holistic approaches for achieving or enhancing physical health is well known. The mind-body connections for well-being in both physical and mental domains are well established from medical and therapeutic studies.

Whatever approach to well-being you select, there is a way to enhance your effectiveness. It involves opening up and accessing more directly your own creativity—your goal-seeking nature—and your natural ability for physical and mental well-being.

How to Begin

Beginning a dedicated *Creative Journal* for charting progress toward goals and well-being is a significant activity for optimizing your achievements and for maintaining health. The first step is to purchase or make a dedicated journal for your adventure into life and health. Give it whatever name you like—*My Creative Journal*, *My Book of Achievements and Well-Being*, or simply, *My Special Journal*. The idea of creativity in this venture is important, since you will be creating a constructive future path *and* a healthier individual. You are creating you; you are creating what you can become.

When you have your *Creative Journal* ready, paste your photograph on the inside cover. This book is yours; you are the objective, the "target person." On page one, write out your objectives and begin. At first, your objective can be very basic, such as " I desire to discover the best direction for my life," or "What specific activity is best for me?" You decide.

For your health objectives, write out "What is best for my physical and psychological well-being?" The overlap between physical and psychological conditions is fundamental, so your activity goals may overlap with your physical or psychological needs or objectives. After recording your basic objectives on page one, you are ready to begin your self-creative exploration.

The next important step is to set aside time periods for impressions or information relevant to your activity goal and your health goal. It may be best to do this at different times. There are two general approaches for exploring; one is to seek insight during periods of relaxation or meditation; another is to seek insight during dreams. Sometimes relaxation states and dream states have similar aspects, especially when dreams become lucid.

Select times for your co-creative journeys when you will be undisturbed. A certain time of the evening or a specific night may be best. Frequency can be increased or decreased as you gain experience.

Goals

During these self-creative periods, you may suddenly have a vision of something you are actually doing—it may seem like watching a movie. Record the specifics in your *Creative Journal*. How did this experience feel? Did you sense a "connection"? Was this depicting a future you? If so, consider ways to achieve that future goal. If it is unclear how best to actually achieve that future, write our a new objective for your relaxing or dreaming state. You may discover that dreaming is the best method for you, since dreams usually have complete story lines and lots of dynamics that give a much better feel of the possible future situation. You may need to devote some time to dream work before you begin your creative journey.

To focus dreams toward your creative objective, simply write it in your journal. Repeat it frequently before sleep, and hold a strong intent to recall the relevant dream that night. You may have many dreams during the night that focus on your objectives. It may help if you intend to remember only the last dream of the night—usually before you wake up naturally—as the dream that responds to your creative objective. It will be easier to recall. Then record it as soon as you can in your *Creative Journal*.

With this approach, you will readily discover the natural and creative impulses and new directions that may have been trying to break into your surface awareness but were suppressed. Then, when you have rehearsed them in waking imagination or in dream experiences and feel that they are really what you want to strive for you are more likely to accomplish them. It is like living ahead in time.

There is another strategy that may be more important than uncovering new objectives or goals. You can enter a relaxed period or seek a dream for rehearsing activities you are currently considering. Discover how they actually feel. Did you like the unfolding imagery or dream dynamics? Did this rehearsal allow you to see your intentions from different perspectives? For example, suppose you plan to pursue a given vocation. Rehearse it. Maybe you feel better in some other field, and your tendency toward a specific vocation or profession is driven by the pressure or expectations of others—and is not best for you.

You may explore very specific activities this way. For example, suppose you are about to begin a new venture with someone you do not know well. Rehearse this emerging situation during relaxation or dreams; does it feel right? As you uncover your psi talents—this usually happens when we begin consistent meditation or dreamwork—you may catch a glimpse of hidden agendas and be able to approach the situation cautiously. Maybe it is best to avoid it entirely.

Well-Being

Your approach to exploring your psychological and physical well-being is similar to that for seeking insight into new activities or goals. Simply write out your well-being objectives, such as "What do I need to know about my health? What can I do to improve my health? What is specifically wrong with my health, and why?" There are many ways to express your well-being objective; choose the most appropriate one for you. The exact way we phrase our well-being concern is not too important; significant insights will surface. We may, for example, intend to seek impressions during relaxing or dreaming that relate to a physical situation and instead have a dream about an activity or relationship issue that has an influence on our health. For example, some individuals recovering from life-threatening illnesses resolve to make significant changes in lifestyle, vocation or relationships, since they have discovered that those situations had a role in weakening their immune system and permitting the illness to progress.

As we seek insight into physical or psychological issues, our meditations or dreams may suggest specific actions, such as diet shift, more exercise, or something more specific like a certain food product or a change in environment. Most of the general impressions will probably track what we already know, but experiencing it directly in meditation or in dreams can have a powerful motivating effect. We somehow know that we have accessed information from beyond our surface knowledge and are more likely to act on the impressions. For example, someone who is trying to break nicotine addiction may have a vivid dream of being consumed by something fearsome—a fire-breathing dragon (a real example). The feeling conveyed is intense and motivates the inner psyche of that individual to abandon the habit. The dreamer has come face to face with an aspect of himself or herself that does not want the dreamer to dribble away his or her life on life-limiting activities. Think how powerful such a vivid dream would be for drug addicts. Excessive alcohol use and addictive drugs throw chemical barricades against pathways into our inner resources and creative talents. Addictions such as these are contra-life and impact on all of us.

When we seek impressions about our physical and mental well-being, we are accessing our subconscious mind that knows the truth. We are the first to know what is wrong with us long before any overt symptoms appear. The advanced detection ability of our immune system is intensive, and we can access the clues that it senses. Imagery during relaxed periods and dreams can be the best early warning method possible for emerging physical illness or psychological disturbances.

As we gain proficiency in searching our wellness landscape, we will be able to respond to the emerging condition well ahead of the time when it becomes critical. For example, during a routine "checkup" on yourself, you may have a surprising dream that shows a spotlight illuminating an area in your lungs (a real example). You should immediately schedule a visit to a competent physician. There are many situations in which you can be the first to know what may be out of balance with your physical or psychological situation. Such information can lead to activity that reverses the situation, and you can then move on to charting new paths for your life.

As in any activity, we need to maintain objectivity and balance in our self-creating activities. Sometimes our biases and expectations get in the way and distort our impressions. With practice, and especially with a dedicated *Creative Journal*, we learn which are distortions and which are authentic. Then we can move on in life with a new partner—our subconscious creative self. We can readily chart the progress of our self-creative achievements and those that lead to our physical/psychological well-being.

As you gain proficiency, you may explore the self-healing potential of visualization and dreams. If you are recovering from an illness or accident, hold firm intentions of being restored to full health. The exact imagery may not be important, as long as the focus is on the goal, not the process. Our subconscious mind can determine the appropriate activities for accelerating recovery. By experiencing lucid dreams or conscious dreams, you can engage in whatever activity is necessary to accelerate recovery. This may mean visualizing yourself being healed through symbolic methods such as being bathed in healing light, or being healed with the aid of a figure that invokes confidence in the healing process.

Continuing Your Journey

A *Creative Journal* provides insight into your creative and healing potentials and how to achieve them.

By seeking to create the path best suited for your journey through life, you align yourself with the deeper co-creative principles of the universe. By giving high priority to your physical and psychological well-being, you optimize what you can actually accomplish and place fewer demands on others—allowing them potentially more freedom to explore their own creative nature.

As you progress, you will automatically discover other aspects of your subconscious nature. You will sense the mysteriousness of life, the environment and the universe—you will become aware of the unity of all things and how you can use your creative talents to help others.

Your *Creative Journal* opens a gateway into the co-creative and evolutionary principles of the universe.

Try Your Psi

φ

This Appendix has a variety of "targets" for practicing your psi talents. Choose any mode comfortable to you for your psi session; you can seek psi impressions during relaxation or dreaming. It does not matter what you label or call your psi effort—psi, ESP, clairvoyance, remote viewing or anything you designate. If no one else is looking at the targets in this Appendix, then the idea of telepathy is not relevant unless you consider telepathy to include your accessing your future knowledge.

Even though the target descriptions are written and are not actual pictures, the approach for you to "access" or "see" them is the same as if they were real pictures. Some targets are simple, others are complex.

I have organized thirty targets in three groups of ten targets each:

Scenes (S) can be natural places or show structures.

People (P) can be individual or group, either static or depicting activity.

Wildlife (W) can be individual or group, either static or depicting activity.

Targets in each group are on a separate page:

Group S, Group P, and Group W

There are ten targets per group on each page, which are identified from top to bottom as follows:

S-1 through S-10 are on Page S.

P-1 through P-10 are on Page P.

W-1 through W-10 are on Page W.

Each target has a separate target designation: S-1, S-2, S-3, and so on. These designators are marked on the left, center and right side of the page above the target descriptions. These descriptions are brief and are kept to the left half of the group page. The separate page identifiers (Group S, Group P, Group W) used for each group are clearly marked close to the *right-hand corner* at the *top* and the *bottom* of each group page, to facilitate locating. This allows you to determine the target *after* you have recorded your impressions without inadvertently seeing it prematurely or glimpsing another target.

Note: None of the target material has unusual emotional content or can be considered negative or threatening.

When you are ready, select group S, P or W. If you select the S group, then your first target is S-1, your second target is S-2, and so on. For your first psi experiment in group S, write "Target = S-1" or "T = S-1" on your paper or in your session notebook. To initiate your psi process, focus on this target designation and fix attention on seeing or experiencing the target. You can write or say, for example, "I desire to receive impressions of Target S-1." Repeat this request to your subconscious mind. You may shorten it to "Target S-1" or "S-1." Other targeting approaches such as "today's target" or simply "target" can be used.

Use a similar approach if you intend to dream the target. Write out your objective, and repeat it frequently before sleep, along with the suggestion to recall the dream upon waking. It helps if you set aside a specific night and seek to have a psi dream during your last dream cycle of the night. This cycle usually occurs immediately prior to waking. Dreams at this time are easier to remember than those that occur earlier.

As you move into your psi session, note and record, when feasible, any impression that comes to you. Maybe it is a fleeting image, a color flash, a feeling or a sensation perhaps of motion. Sketch whatever you can. If you do not visualize well, then simply write a few words about any fleeting thought or word that may have come to you. Maybe you felt something. But do *not* analyze your impressions or try to give them a specific name. Your analytical mind wants to nudge your impressions into something specific that may cause you to drift way off course. Simply record them as if you were a detached observer.

After you have completed your psi session, which may last 15-30 minutes, review your notes and add anything that you did not record earlier. Maybe certain memories or associations come to mind.

With practice, you will discover that your impressions become easier to recall and identify. It is helpful if you make a list of your general and specific impressions. That will help you learn the difference between your impressions and what may be your analytical mind intruding prematurely. Also note in what target group or aspect you do best; maybe it is shapes or colors; maybe it is scenes, or people or wildlife.

After you have recorded your waking relaxed state or dream impressions, go discover ground truth. To do this, simply peel back *only the corners* of the next few pages to locate the correct target group.

When you have the correct page, insert a file holder or thick $8\frac{1}{2}$" × 11" sheet of colored paper between the pages and slide it up until it completely covers the page. For group S targets, for example, locate the "S" page and insert the sheet of paper, being sure the entire page is covered. Then open the book to that covered page and slowly slide this loose paper down until you note "S-1" on the left, middle and right side at the top of the page. Immediately below "S-1" on the left side of the page is a description of your target. Slide the page a few lines further so you can read the description of Target S-1. Do not slide the loose page any lower, or you will be entering S-2's territory. In your next session (for Target S-2), repeat this page-uncovering procedure, but slide your covering page to S-2 in order to reveal its description. Follow the same feedback procedure for targets in groups P and W.

When you receive feedback, compare results to your impressions. Note what features correlated—shapes, colors, and so on, along with any impressions you had correct. Keep a track record to see in what target groups or target aspects you did best. This will give you an idea of your psi cognitive style and preferences and give insight into how reliable you can be for future psi projects of different types.

You may want to try a precognition experiment. To do this, write out all the thirty designators of S-1 through W-10 on 3" × 5" cards, one designator per card. Shuffle them and set them aside until after your precognition session.

Then enter your psi session, intending to see or access the target shown on the card to be selected. Your targeting instruction or request can be "I desire to access the next target to be selected." Or "I desire to see the future target." Or "I desire to see the target approaching me in my future," or something similar.

After you have recorded your impressions, randomly select a card from your target pool of thirty 3" × 5" cards (or have a colleague select the card). If the card is W-6, for example, and your impressions were generally of wildlife, then you will immediately know you have the correct target category. To receive specific feedback, have a colleague open to the Group W page and read (or write out) the description of target W-6. Compare this to the impressions that you have recorded and see if you have perceived the correct type of wildlife.

This Appendix offers you the opportunity to explore your psi talents at your leisure. You can vary your approach as you progress. Try a mix of relaxed and dreaming modes to see what works best for you. Keep good records and pay close attention to the sketches you make.

φ φ φ

Now you are ready for S-1. Take a few months to work through to P-10. I am interested in your results. Contact me by email at: baygraff@chesapeake.net

Targets—Group S

S - 1   **S - 1**   S - 1
Yosemite National Park with a clear view
of a waterfall from ground level.

S - 2   **S - 2**   S - 2
A Mayan temple with a clear view of the
steps from ground level.

S - 3   **S - 3**   S - 3
A wide, flat tundra scene showing hundreds
of tundra polygons (from freezing and
thawing) in a predominately green setting.

S - 4   **S - 4**   S - 4
A telescopic view of the full moon with
craters and mountain features.

S - 5   **S - 5**   S - 5
A large saguaro cactus from ground level.

S - 6   **S - 6**   S - 6
Mt. Fuji from a distance. Its conical snow
covered peak is clear.

S - 7   **S - 7**   S - 7
Statue of Liberty in New York City.

S - 8   **S - 8**   S - 8
The Gateway Arch at St. Louis, MO, as seen
from across the Mississippi.

S - 9   **S - 9**   S - 9
The gothic cathedral of Notre Dame in
Paris, France.

S - 10   **S - 10**   S - 10
Breaking surf along the Maine coast with a
sailboat nearby.

Targets—Group P

P - 1 **P - 1** **P - 1**
Face of a clown smiling and laughing, like Red Skelton.

P - 2 **P - 2** **P - 2**
Abraham Lincoln; typical pose with flat-top high hat.

P - 3 **P - 3** **P - 3**
A woman performing a complex figure-skating pattern.

P - 4 **P - 4** **P - 4**
Close-up view of a Native American medicine man with feathers and rattles.

P - 5 **P - 5** **P - 5**
Dorothy in *The Wizard of Oz* walking with the Tin Man and Scarecrow.

P - 6 **P - 6** **P - 6**
Martin Luther King delivering a moving speech.

P - 7 **P - 7** **P - 7**
An infant lying in a crib, sleeping.

P - 8 **P - 8** **P - 8**
A robust St. Patrick's Day parade with drums and bugle music.

P - 9 **P - 9** **P - 9**
A bowling game with a man approaching the line about to release a bowling ball.

P - 10 **P - 10** **P - 10**
Action scene of any tennis game.

Targets—Group W

W - 1   **W - 1**   **W - 1**
A goldfish swirling in a bowl.

W - 2   **W - 2**   **W - 2**
A parrot squawking.

W - 3   **W - 3**   **W - 3**
An eagle swoops from the sky.

W - 4   **W - 4**   **W - 4**
A beaver gnaws at a tree.

W - 5   **W - 5**   **W - 5**
A small puppy with soft brown fur.

W - 6   **W - 6**   **W - 6**
A herd of zebras moving from left to right.

W - 7   **W - 7**   **W - 7**
A kitten playing with a ball of string.

W - 8   **W - 8**   **W - 8**
A raccoon splashing in a stream.

W - 9   **W - 9**   **W - 9**
A kangaroo hopping down a road.

W - 10   **W - 10**   **W - 10**
A huge white whale, like Moby Dick,
breaking and spouting water.

Endnotes

1 *Thoughts Through Space*, by Harold Sherman and Sir Hubert Wilkins, describes how Harold Sherman tracked the activities of Sir Hubert Wilkins for six months in 1937–1938 during a marathon ESP experiment while Sir Hubert was flying search missions for a missing Soviet airplane in the Arctic (see Resources).

2 A summary of his results is given in *Tracks in the Psychic Wilderness*, Chapter 6, "Arctic Search."

3 *Tracks in the Psychic Wilderness* provides additional background on remote viewing.

4 This classic work is described in *Dream Telepathy* (see Resources).

5 Other accounts of fire premonition can be found in *Dreams That Come True*, by Ryback and Sweitzer.

6 *Tracks in the Psychic Wilderness*, Chapter 9, "Trouble in Reactor Bay."

7 *Tracks in the Psychic Wilderness*, Chapter 1, "Ohio Caverns."

8 *The Psychic Search*, page 21–28, "Lost Aircraft."

9 In 1985, this remote viewing unit was transferred to DIA as part of STARGATE— the integrated research and applications remote viewing project under management of DIA. STARGATE was discontinued in 1995, two years after I retired.

10 *The Psychic Search*, Pages 38–39, "Cross-Country Kidnapping."

11 This information is in public records.

12 *Tracks in the Psychic Wilderness*, Chapter 9, "Trouble in Reactor Bay."

13 A hologram is formed from interference patterns of interacting electromaganetic radiation, such as coherent light waves. When the recorded pattern is illuminated by the same type of light, an image of the original object or scene appears. Even a small portion of the hologram has the same information as the larger original, although it is not as accurate.

14 *The Way of the Explorer*, Chapter 2, "Sea of Sky."

15 *Conjuring Up Philip*, by Owen and Sparrow.

16 *The Way of the Explorer*, Chapter 10, "The Forward Future."

17 I was employed at the Foreign Technology Division (FTD) at Wright Patterson Air Force Base when the fantasy of twelve little green men being held captive in the basement was originated. I wanted to run an advertisement in the local paper for twelve little green women to keep them company!

18 There has been, and still is, a considerable amount of confusion caused by terms used to describe psi phenomena. For example: Some data thought to be from remote viewing may include telepathy (direct mind contact). Some data thought to be from telepathy may include direct psi contact with the environment (remote viewing, clairvoyance). The Glossary has details on terminology.

Glossary

Clairvoyance   An old term associated with extrasensory perception (ESP), whereby information is obtained directly from the environment without the mediation of the physical senses. Someone else's knowledge, accessed via telepathy, is not considered to be involved. Clairvoyance is similar to remote viewing. In practice, it is difficult to identify the source of ESP information. In many instances, the information could have been derived via a telepathic process.

Conscious Dream   A dream in which you are aware of being in a dream and aware that you are dreaming. "Lucid dream" has the same meaning.

Extrasensory Perception (ESP)   A term made popular by Dr. J. B. Rhine in the early 1930s. It refers to an ability to access information via an unknown mental process.

Field Theory   A concept in physics that considers all physical phenomena as resulting from an interaction with a property of space or spacetime.

Hologram   A film that records interference patterns resulting from the interaction of light, usually coherent, or other electromagnetic waves. A reference beam is combined with a beam reflected from the objects to be recorded, creating an interference pattern of light and dark areas. When the film is developed and illuminated by the original reference beam, the objects are recreated as an image that can be seen. A small portion of the hologram contains the same information as the original, though it is not as accurate.

Intuition   An act of knowing without using the usual rational processes. It has two aspects: (1) subconscious recognition of patterns in known information, (2) integration of known data with subliminal and ESP information.

Nonlocal Phenomenon   Term from quantum physics that refers to a quantum-level coupling that exists between elementary particles. This interaction is instantaneous and not limited by distance. When particles are separated, a change to one instantly affects the other, no matter how far apart they are.

Parapsychology   Experimental science that studies psi phenomena from a scientific point of view.

Precognition   An aspect of ESP that allows the perception of probable future events or situations that cannot be deduced from available data.

Psi   Psi, or Ψ, is the twenty-third letter of the Greek alphabet. Pronounced "sigh," it is a neutral term for mental phenomena that include informational (e.g., ESP, remote viewing) and energetic or action effects (e.g., psychokinesis).

Psychokinesis (PK)   The ability to mentally influence or interact with sensitive devices or the environment.

Quantum   Quantum, or quanta, refers to the *smallest* unit of energy that can be emitted or absorbed by matter. It is a fundamental aspect of the physical universe.

Recurrent Spontaneous Psychokinesis (RSPK)   Term used to describe frequent PK effects that occur spontaneously. An older term, poltergeist phenomenon, is also used to describe these spontaneous energetic events.

Remote Viewing (RV)   A mental ability related to ESP used to access distant or shielded information. Other similar terms: remote perception, enhanced perception. RV was originally used in the context of an experimental procedure. As practiced, it resembles clairvoyance, although a telepathic aspect cannot be excluded. The term "remote viewing" was coined in the early 1970s as a neutral term to eliminate the biases and troublesome images often associated with older terms such as clairvoyance. RV can be visual in character—revealing natural or structural features—or may involve other sensory modes such as feelings, sound, smell, taste or touch.

Some remote viewing practitioners advocate that remote viewing only occurs when rigid protocols are observed. Of course proper procedures and evaluation methods are required to validate *any* form of psi data. Other practitioners promote the idea that certain techniques or strategies *must* be followed for remote viewing to occur. This is an erroneous viewpoint and is probably emphasized for marketing purposes only. Most of these techniques are based on an arbitrary progression and on strict adherence to how the objective is defined. These techniques are not inherent in the basic phenomenon and can lead to unnecessary and confusing complexity.

Subliminal Perception   Sensory impressions that are below the threshold of conscious awareness.

Synchronicity   Meaningful coincidences that often are mediated by subconscious psi activity. Our intuitive/psi faculty is constantly scanning the field of future probabilities and nudges our paths into meaningful intersections when feasible.

Telepathy   An older term that originally referred to ESP sensing of someone else's feelings. It has been expanded to include sensing of any information known to someone else via psi.

Resources

Bohm, David. *Wholeness and the Implicate Order*. London: Routledge & Kegan Paul, 1983.

Bosnak, Robert. *Tracks in the Wilderness Of Dreaming*. New York: Delacorte Press, 1996.

Broughton, Richard. *Parapsychology—The Controversial Science*. New York: Ballantine, 1991.

Delaney, Gale. *New Directions in Dream Interpretation*. Albany, NY: State University of New York Press, 1995.

Duncan, Lois and William Roll. *Psychic Connections*. New York: Delacorte, 1995.

Garfield, Patricia. *Creative Dreaming*. New York: Ballantine, 1974.

Garfield, Patricia. *The Healing Power of Dreams*. New York: Simon & Schuster, 1991.

Graff, Dale. *Tracks in the Psychic Wilderness*. Boston, MA: Element, 1998.

Harrison, Shirley and Lynn Franklin. *The Psychic Search*. Portland, ME: Gannett Publishing, 1981.

Hartman, Ernest. *Boundaries in the Mind*. New York: Basic Books, 1991.

Hibbard, Whitney and Raymond Worring. *Psychic Criminology*. Springfield, IL: Charles C. Thomas, 1982.

Jahn, Robert and Brenda Dunne. *Margins of Reality; The Role of Consciousness in the Physical World*. San Diego, CA: Harcourt Brace & Co., 1987.

Jung, Carl, G. *Flying Saucers: A Modern Myth of Things Seen in the Skies*. Princeton, NJ: Princeton University Press, 1978.

Jung, Carl, G. *Dreams*. Princeton, NJ: Bollinger, 1974.

LaBerge, Stephen. *Exploring the World of Lucid Dreams*. New York: Ballantine, 1990.

Lyons, Arthur and Marcello Truzzi. *The Blue Sense*. New York: Warner Books, 1991.

Mitchell, Edgar. *The Way of the Explorer*. New York: Putnam, 1996.

Moss, Robert. *Dreamgates*. New York: Three Rivers Press, 1998.

Owen, Iris and Margaret Sparrow. *Conjuring Up Philip*. New York: Harper & Row, 1976.

Puthoff, Harold and Russell Targ. *Mind Reach*. New York: Delacorte Press, 1977.

Radin, Dean. *The Conscious Universe*. San Francisco: HarperCollins, 1997.

Rhine, Louisa E. *ESP in Life and Lab*. Toronto: Collier Macmillan Books, 1967.

Rhine, Louisa E. *The Invisible Picture: A Study of Psychic Experiences*. Jefferson, NC: McFarland, 1981.

Rhine, Louisa E. *Hidden Channels of the Mind*. New York: William Morrow and Company, 1961.

Ryback, David and Letitia Sweitzer. *Dreams That Come True*. New York: Doubleday, 1988.

Sheldrake, Rupert. *A New Science of Life*. London: HarperCollins, 1995.

Sherman, Harold and Sir Hubert Wilkins. *Thoughts Through Space*. Amherst, WI: Amherst Press, 1983.

Siegel, Alan B. *Dreams that Can Change Your Life*. New York: Berkley Books, 1990.

Talbot, Michael. *The Holographic Universe*, New York: HarperCollins, 1991.

Targ, Russell and Keith Harary. *The Mind Race*. New York: Ballantine, 1984.

Tart, Charles T. *Body Mind Spirit: Exploring the Parapsychology of Spirituality*. Charlottesville, VA: Hampton Roads, 1997.

Ullman, Montague, Stanley Krippner and Alan Vaughn. *Dream Telepathy*. New York: Penguin Books, 1974.

Ullman, Montague and Nan Zimmerman. *Working with Dreams*. New York: Delacorte, 1979.

Van de Castle, Robert. *Our Dreaming Mind*. New York: Ballantine Books, 1994.

BAYCLIFF PSI SEMINARS

Web Site: http://www.chesapeake.net/~baygraff/

About the Author

Dale Graff is an internationally recognized lecturer and writer on psi topics. He is a physicist and a former director of Project STARGATE, the government program for research and applications of remote viewing phenomena. His media appearances include ABC's *Nightline*, *Good Morning America*, CNN, *FOX Crier Report*, *Voice of America*, and a variety of television documentaries, including the Discovery and Arts and Entertainment (A & E) channels. His extensive explorations into intuition, extrasensory perception (ESP), remote viewing, synchronicity and precognition provide a varied experiential background for his psi activities.

He presents workshops and seminars for individuals and small groups through BAYCLIFF PSI SEMINARS in Southern Maryland and other organizations in the United States, Canada and Europe.

BAYCLIFF PSI SEMINARS presents an integrated approach for psi exploration that emphasizes balance and well-being. Dale provides user-friendly guidance and explanation of psychic abilities for people who seek to expand their talents or understand their experiences. Dream seminars focus on future-seeing and healing potential.

For information about seminars contact Dale Graff at:

Email: baygraff@chesapeake.net

Web Site: http://www.chesapeake.net/~baygraff/

Mail: Dale Graff
168 Windcliff Road
Prince Frederick, MD 20678-4303

Note: Dale welcomes accounts of psi experiences from readers.